The Virtues *of* Suffering

How to Seek God's Glory in Your Afflictions

Glendon and Maureen Watson

◆ FriesenPress

Suite 300 - 990 Fort St
Victoria, BC, V8V 3K2
Canada

www.friesenpress.com

ISBN
978-1-5255-5318-9 (Hardcover)
978-1-5255-5319-6 (Paperback)
978-1-5255-5320-2 (eBook)

1. *Religion, Christian Life, Death, Grief, Bereavement*

Distributed to the trade by The Ingram Book Company

The
Virtues
of
Suffering

Pastor Bob,
God's Mantle of
Apostolic Anointing is open preparing
your Life for the Church to be the
ushering in the Coming of Our Lord
Jesus Christ.

Jan 26 1 2020

TABLE OF CONTENTS

Foreword

The Virtues of Suffering by Glendon and Maureen Watson

Wow... what a great book! I am so glad you picked it up. Authors, Glendon and Maureen Watson do an impeccable job at tackling complex questions concerning suffering. People do suffer and sometimes their suffering is intense and extreme. Trouble will come in this life, and it has the potential to tear us apart, to render us weak and helpless. From our perspective, there is not always an answer to why. This book offers answers to the "why" question.

When we understand why, it helps us to endure the suffering. Yes, there are reasons. This book offers scriptural proof to what might be otherwise shrouded in mystery. The authors remind us of the man Job. They explain that Job is not just an example to follow, but his life teaches us that God's people do and will suffer in this world. Becoming a Christian and believing in Jesus Christ does not make you exempt from suffering.

I am grateful for Glendon and Maureen insight and inspiration on this subject. I know this book will bring revelation and instruction to help you make sense of suffering.

Pastor Bob Johnston
Lead Pastor: Global Kingdom Ministries, Toronto ON

Suffering is a topic that many of us have avoided with some reluctance to talk or write about.

Glendon and Maureen have been inspired to write this book based on their sound knowledge of the Bible and a wealth of firsthand experience of personal suffering.

Zooming into a careful navigation of the issues of the life of Job, his friend's response and God's answers to them, Glendon and Maureen give us their convincing perspective, as persons whom have suffered greatly and have seen the magnificent hand of God rescuing them. They show us through multiple scriptures, how we too can trust the Almighty God to give us joy in the midst of suffering.

Through Job's response to God, the authors show us that 'God can do all things...' so whatever He does is wrapped up with His wise 'purpose'. Just as Job and his friend's attitude and understanding had changed, we too can be transformed in our lives as we follow Job's story and realize that God did not leave Job in his suffering. Job finished well, far greater than he started spiritually, mentally, emotionally and physically.

Glendon and Maureen have shown us that suffering is the price that we pay for success. God's pruning and purging of our lives brings fruitfulness and maturity.

Reading this-power packed book, with many carefully selected scriptures, can change our perspective from fear of inevitable suffering to welcoming with a new understanding like Job and Apostle Paul and also embrace the grace and comfort that God provides in the midst of our suffering.

This book should be read by anyone who experienced suffering and came out battered and bruised and have difficulty answering the question, "Why God? How could this happen to me?", and also by students of the Word, and anyone who loves and cares for the many people around us who are suffering.

Dr. Dudley Mayers
Director, Kingdom Bible Training Center.
Chaplain, Global Chaplaincy Center

It is an honor to write a foreword for this insightful book. As a believer, I am aware that the importance of the subject, Virtues of Suffering, cannot be overemphasized. This is most likely why the authors, Glendon and Maureen have chosen to write about this very important subject that is much needed in Christendom. For the edification of the soul and as a testament to the faithfulness, purpose and supremacy of God.

The authors, have hearts for the word of God. This was quite evident in Glendon's first book, "Demons and Devils, How they Enter - 2015", and even more evident in this epic work that focuses on the intriguing subject of suffering and its virtues. The Bible is very clear on this subject as it is described as a rite of passage for every born- again Christian to get into the Kingdom of God. The Bible says in the Book of Acts that through many tribulations we must enter the Kingdom of God. (Acts 14:22) This is reiterated in Matthew 10:22, "You will be hated by everyone on account of my name, but the one who perseveres to the end will be saved".

King David, the man after God's own heart, lamented his lot in psalms 6:3. Even he, a royalty was not spared the agony of suffering. He cried, "My soul is in anguish. How long O Lord, how long?" Through suffering, the Christian is made whole and stronger in his or her faith. Therefore, suffering is an integral aspect of the Christian journey on earth as he or she awaits the second coming of our Lord Jesus Christ. It is important to ask the fundamental question of how suffering came into the world after God created a perfect world described as a masterpiece. The answer is sin as eloquently discussed by the authors. The fall of man in the Garden of Eden resulted in sin, and suffering came as a consequence. In Genesis 3, we learned how the deceit by Satan of Eve led to the disobedience to God after she ate the forbidden fruit and passed it on to Adam. Thus, suffering became the end result of their sin. The Bible stated in Genesis 3:7-10, that they suffered shame and fear, and the suffering continues today each time we disobey God.

With the supreme power of God and His ability to stop the suffering of His children, one may wonder why He still allows His children to suffer. In some cases they are subjected to imprisonment, severe bodily affliction and even death. The authors' proffers very pertinent answers with their critical and discerning delve into the subject of the virtues of suffering, specifically examining four core aspects; 1) Why do we suffer? 2) What is God's position on the subject of suffering? 3) Why does He allow it? And 4) Are there any benefits to suffering?

The authors have done this with tact, finesse and the leading of the Holy Spirit while supporting his assertions and claims with the appropriate biblical references and illustrations. The author rightfully stated that our suffering as Christians which according to Apostle Paul in II Corinthians is multifaceted and can come in various forms, is not ad hoc, but designed for the strengthening of faith and the glorification of God.

The authors illustrated his cogent points with the story of Job in the Bible who was afflicted with pain and suffering and suffered untold persecution and torture at the hands of Satan. The salient lessons in Job's suffering are too hard to ignore, and the authors presented those lessons seamlessly so the reader may understand and appreciate the veracity of the subject. God used his situation to counter Satan's claim that self-serving desires are the prime motivations for humans. Out of Job's suffering came the revelation that humans, among other things, are motivated by godly affairs and not solely by the need for self-aggrandizement and self-adulation.

Thus, Job's unjust suffering reminds us that God in His infinite wisdom allows His children, the righteous, to be tried. The author states that it is only through persecution and trials that a Christian can truly be affirmed in his or her faith. The Bible states in Psalm 11: 4-5, The Lord is in His holy temple, the Lord's throne is in heaven; His eyes behold, His eyelids test the sons of men. The Lord tests the righteous. To this effect, many of the disciples who gave up their professional and personal lives to follow the Lord were tested and killed. James' martyrdom was recorded in the Bible in Acts 12:1-3, and was the first of the twelve disciples to be martyred by way of beheading. Peter was crucified upside down while Paul was also beheaded. Other disciples suffered similar fate.

It is imperative for Christians to understand the virtues of suffering as brilliantly discussed by the author. In Job's example used extensively by the author, Job realized that God was in complete control of his situation and though he suffered tremendous hardship, he learned to trust God and put his faith in Him. The central lesson in this book, Virtues of Suffering, is that God wants us to trust Him no matter the trial and persecution we are enduring. He wants us to know that our suffering is not in vain and it is well within His will. Though we may not understand the reason or the purpose why He allows the righteous to be tested, we must accept His will in our lives as Christians and pray for strength and God's favor in times of trial. The Bible says in Isaiah 55:8-9, "For my thoughts are not your thoughts, neither are your ways my ways. As the heavens are higher than the earth, so are my ways higher than your ways and my thoughts than your thoughts".

As Brother Watson and his dear wife Maureen have shared their deep knowledge of the subject through this medium, I pray that the Lord will manifest His enduring word in your life as espoused in this book

Be blessed.

Professor Philip Alalibo
Department of Humanities & Social Sciences
Coordinator, General Education & Liberal Studies
Centennial College of Applied

The Virtues of Suffering

Why do we suffer?
What is God saying?
Where is He in all of this?
Are there benefits to your suffering?

Preface

Between 2003 and 2006, I lost four of my closest family members—my father, my brother, my sister, and her daughter. Additionally, since I began writing this book in 2015, I have lost over six family members and close friends due to illnesses. These experiences of death and intense suffering have further aroused my curiosity about this topic and served as the impetus for this book.

On April 27, 2015, over 4,000 people died in an earthquake in Nepal. Aftershocks occurred, and the number of deaths continued to rise. Undoubtedly, Christians were among the many who died, and surviving family members included Christians and non-Christians. Both groups suffered as a result of that catastrophe.

Suffering is not unique to any people, place, or time. Suffering and death come from the disobedience of our fore parents. If the first man, Adam, had stood his ground in the Garden of Eden, none of us would have been in this predicament.

Repeatedly, I have faced suffering through physical attack, sickness, and the sickness and death of others. God has used these experiences to inspire the writing of this book. I believe that at some point in time, subconsciously or otherwise, many people ask the question: "Lord, why do I have to suffer or even die?" To understand sickness, the effects of diseases, or even death, one must first understand the process that leads to death. God gave me a glimpse of the process of death, and within the process lies the ultimate purpose. The Bible says that to everything there is a purpose.

Apart from the biblical injunction that death is the wages of sin, there is some "method to the madness," as some would say. There is a purpose for everything under the sun.

Death is a passageway, an integral part of a great story, and to understand it, we must first understand the significance of the process leading up to it. Why the suffering, the pains, and sorrows of life? For the Christian, death should be the happiest time of his/her life. Why? you might ask. Because it's the final enemy to be defeated in life. God has designed our suffering and eventual death to work together for our good. In fact, the Bible says,

> "Precious in the sight of the Lord is the death of his saints"
> (Psalm 116:15 KJV)

Whether or not we glory in tribulation like Paul, the apostle, or have joy in our suffering, is predicated on our understanding and embracing of the virtues of suffering. We'll never be able to endure hardship as good soldiers of the cross of Calvary without first understanding the content of this book, *The Virtues of Suffering*. This acknowledgment and embracing of what suffering brings to the lives of believers caused Paul to write in 2 Corinthians 4:17: *"For our light affliction, which is but for a moment, worketh for us a far more exceeding and eternal weight of glory."* For this same reason, it is said about Jesus, *"who for the joy that was set before him endured the cross, despising the shame"* (Hebrews 12:2a, KJV). May we encounter the grace of suffering as we read and understand. May we also be willing to embrace the virtues of suffering illustrated in this book.

Acknowledgment

Thanks be to God our Father and the Lord Jesus Christ for Their unsurpassed generosity. Thanks for the development of my mind, for many visions, illuminations, revelations, understandings, and insights that our God has brought to bear upon me in preparation for this writing. Truly our God is amazing.

Thanks to our senior pastor, Rev. Bob Johnston, of Global Kingdom Ministries, Toronto, for feeding me with the Word of God each Sunday. He has brought home to me the simplicity of the gospel and confirmed many revelations that God has placed in my heart on the subject of suffering and humility. His graphic depiction of Christ's humility in suffering has illuminated the significance of humbling ourselves under God's mighty hand.

Thanks to my wife, my mother, and my daughter. They have stood with me in the best as well as the worst of times. They have helped me withstand the trials and tribulations I experienced while writing this book. I have known God's comfort through my loved ones at home. They have been my nurses, prayer partners, and providers.

To all others who have impacted this writing in one way or another, I say thank you. I have learned a lot just by seeing others going through their own struggles, trials, and tribulations.

The following books, magazines articles, and teachings are acknowledged:

Oswald Chambers, *My Utmost for His Highest,* (Dodd Mead & Co.), 1935

LifeChurch.tv, *Finding Comfort in Pain,* 2016

–Chris Oyakhilome, *Healing from Heaven*: Volume 3, (Love World Publishing), 2013

David Prince - Invisible Barriers to Healing: Derrick Prince Ministries. 1989

Special thanks to Rev. Gaetane Marshall (prophetess), whom God has used to help train my ears to hear in the spirit, and my eyes to see into the supernatural.

Special thanks to Prophet TB Joshua, Senior Pastor, SCOAN ministry, whose ministry is broadcasted on YouTube through Emmanuel Television. He has taught me that we aren't characterized by our trials and tribulations. Like Paul the apostle, he often encouraged us to understand that God's strength is made perfect in our weakness. Our level of spirituality isn't determined by the things we suffer, but by our attitude. It's our attitude that determines our altitude in God.

Chapter One: Understanding Your Frailty

The battle for the seeds of God's creation, mankind, is gruesome. It's a battle of life or death, of heaven or hell. God's ultimate desire for mankind is that we be eternally saved to be with Him in His kingdom on earth, and ultimately in heaven. The devil, on the other hand, has a diabolic scheme to bring us to hell with him, where we will encounter the full brunt of fire and torment. The battle begins in the minds of individuals, where the ability to choose is born.

Life is a combination of choices. But are our choices based on the knowledge of God and His kingdom? The Bible says that the soul that commits sin shall surely die (Ezekiel 18:20). This implies that there are consequences when we sin. In other words, sin must be punished. There is a legal requirement for the punishment of man's sin. This is captured in the story of Adam and Eve in the Garden of Eden.

> "The Lord God took the man and put him in the Garden of Eden to work it and take care of it. And the Lord God commanded the man, "You are free to eat from any of the tree in the garden; but you must not eat from the tree of the knowledge of good and evil, for when you eat of it you will surely die." (Genesis 2:15–17)

The Garden was man's home, and God had made it perfect for our dwelling. All Adam had to do was maintain it and live in obedience to God's command. By God's grace, man could do almost anything he wanted, except for one thing … yet he fell for it. Adam and Eve were commanded not to eat the forbidden fruit.

Due to sin, man was appointed to die once, after which he would face judgment: *"And as it is appointed unto men once to die, but after this the judgment"* (Hebrews 9:27, KJV). What a tremendous weakness to obey the voice of a serpent instead of the voice of God. *What frailty!*

Whether you're a believer in Jesus Christ going through trials and tribulations, or a non-believer encountering your own sufferings, understanding suffering can lead you into the greater glory of God for your life.

Paul said in Romans 5:3–8 (KJV):

> "And not only so, but we glory in tribulations also: knowing that tribulation worketh patience; and patience, experience; and experience, hope: And hope maketh not ashamed; because the love of God is shed abroad in our hearts by the Holy Ghost which is given unto us. For when we were yet without strength, in due time Christ died for the ungodly. For scarcely for a righteous man will one die: yet peradventure for a good man some would even dare to die. But God commendeth his love toward us, in that, while we were yet sinners, Christ died for us."

We all face suffering for different reasons; however, God intends our suffering to draw us closer to Him so that we can receive His redemption. Jesus didn't die for the righteous but for sinners, that all might receive redemption through His blood. As a result, our suffering will reveal the weaknesses of our own flesh as well as the condition of our heart, causing us to cry out to a loving and eternal God. What we do with our suffering can either make us better or bitter. God intends for us to understand that all suffering is a result of the fall in the Garden of Eden, but Jesus gave His life that we might have life and have it more abundantly. Only He can deliver us from suffering and save our souls from hell. He is the only way of redemption and to our Father in heaven. Jesus said, *"I am the way"* (John 14:6).

Irrespective of what religion you belong to, Jesus alone can rescue you from all your troubles and bring you safely to our heavenly Father. Some may even die, because the Lord takes them home to save them from evil. God knows just how much evil each person can endure before they fall into unpardonable sin. They are taken away to be spared from evil.

> "The righteous perisheth, and no man layeth it to heart: and merciful men are taken away, none considering that the righteous is taken away from the evil to come. He shall enter into peace: they shall rest in their beds, each one walking in his uprightness." Isaiah 57:1–2 (KJV)

The dispensation of God's grace through our Lord and Savior Jesus Christ does not alter His prerogative to take us home early at times.

In the Lord's model prayer (Matthew 6:9–13), Jesus says, "*And lead us not into temptation, but deliver us from the evil one*" (v. 13, KJV). The inclusion of a request for God not to lead us into temptation teaches us that avoiding temptation should be one of the chief concerns for the Christian. Essentially, we're asking our heavenly Father to lead us away from evil. This petition reflects the believer's desire to avoid the danger of sin altogether. It's to be understood in the sense of permitting us to sin. In this context, it implies that God has control over the tempter to be able to save us from his power if we call upon our heavenly Father.

The word "temptation" can also refer to trials. We know from 1 Corinthians 10:13 that God won't test us beyond our spiritual ability and will always provide a way out. But God might subject us to trials that expose us to Satan's assault for His own purposes, as in the cases of Job and Peter.

> "And the Lord said, Simon, Simon, behold, Satan hath desired to have you, that he may sift you as wheat: But I have prayed for thee, that thy faith fail not: and when thou art converted, strengthen thy brethren" (Luke 22:31–32, KJV).

3

As long as we're in submission to the will of our God, we can humbly ask to be delivered from temptation and for the strength to endure it when it comes.

Whether we're asking God to deliver us from sin or from difficult trials, our goal is to be delivered from the evil one. God might choose to take us home to be with Him to deliver us from impending evil: *"Precious in the eyes of the Lord is the death of His saints..."* (Psalm 116:15 KJV).

God made us so that we must depend upon Him or we will never survive this life or the one to come. Even though we were made in the image and likeness of God, we were made earthen vessels as well.

> "For God, who commanded the light to shine out of darkness, hath shined in our hearts, to give the light of the knowledge of the glory of God in the face of Jesus Christ. But we have this treasure in earthen vessels, that the excellency of the power may be of God, and not of us. We are troubled on every side, yet not distressed; we are perplexed, but not in despair; Persecuted, but not forsaken; cast down, but not destroyed; Always bearing about in the body the dying of the Lord Jesus, that the life also of Jesus might be made manifest in our body. For we which live are always delivered unto death for Jesus' sake, that the life also of Jesus might be made manifest in our mortal flesh. So then death worketh in us, but life in you."
> (2 Corinthians 4:6–12, KJV)

Although the reference was made to Paul, it stands to reason that once you're a child of God, you will encounter similar experiences in life. In our sufferings, trials, temptations, and even persecutions, we participate in Jesus's suffering and death. The Bible said that if we suffer with Him, we will also rise with Him.

The choice is always ours: we either suffer with Christ as Christians, or we suffer without Him. In the former case, we will be rewarded, while in the latter, there is no reward but rather greater punishment to come.

All flesh is as grass.

"The voice said, Cry. And he said, What shall I cry? All flesh is grass, and all the goodliness thereof is as the flower of the field: The grass withereth, the flower fadeth: because the spirit of the Lord bloweth upon it: surely the people is grass. The grass withereth, the flower fadeth: but the word of our God shall stand for ever." (Isaiah 40:6–8, KJV)

God's judgment on wickedness is described as the summer wind that blows on the grass and dries it up. But we have full assurance of the reliability, stability, and eternal nature of His divine words. God's eternal Word stands forever. We must rely upon it for our freedom. God's only begotten Son fulfills His Word. Jesus is the Living Word that lives forever.

"Think not that I am come to destroy the law, or the prophets: I am not come to destroy, but to fulfil. For verily I say unto you, Till heaven and earth pass, one jot or one tittle shall in no wise pass from the law, till all be fulfilled. Whosoever therefore shall break one of these least commandments, and shall teach men so, he shall be called the least in the kingdom of heaven: but whosoever shall do and teach them, the same shall be called great in the kingdom of heaven. (Matthew 5:17–19, KJV).

In the beginning was the Word, and the Word was with God, and the Word was God. The same was in the beginning with God. All things were made by him; and without him was not anything made that was made. In him was life; and the life was the light of men. And the light shineth in darkness; and the darkness comprehended it not. There was a man sent from God, whose name was John. The same came for a witness, to bear witness of the Light that all men through him might believe. He was not that Light, but was sent to bear witness of that Light. That was the true Light, which lighteth every man that cometh into the world. He was in the world, and the world was made by him, and the world knew him not. He came unto his own, and his own received him not. But as many as received him, to them gave he power to become the sons of God, even to them that believe on his name: Which were born, not of blood, nor of the will of the flesh, nor of the will of man, but of God. And the Word was made flesh, and dwelt among us, (and we beheld his glory, the glory as of the only begotten of the Father,) full of grace and truth. John bare witness of him, and cried, saying, this was he of whom I spake, He that cometh after me is preferred before me: for he was before me. And of his fulness have all we received, and grace for grace. For the law was given by Moses, but grace and truth came by Jesus Christ. No man hath seen God at any time; the only begotten Son, which is in the bosom of the Father, he hath declared him." (John 1:1–18, KJV)

Suffering turns our attention not just toward our present, but also toward our future. In their suffering, believers groan with longing for the glorious future in heaven.

"For we know that the whole creation groaneth and travaileth in pain together until now. And not only they, but ourselves also, which have the firstfruits of the Spirit, even we ourselves groan within ourselves, waiting for the adoption, to wit, the redemption of our body. For we are saved by hope: but hope that is seen is not hope: for what a man seeth, why doth he yet hope for?" (Romans 8:22–23, KJV).

Suffering causes sinners and Christians alike to cease from sin, because it helps to slay the flesh that allows for the sinfulness of mankind:

"Forasmuch then as Christ hath suffered for us in the flesh, arm yourselves likewise with the same mind: for he that hath suffered in the flesh hath ceased from sin" (1 Peter 4:1, KJV).

Suffering, whether through pain, sickness, or death of a loved one, challenges every state of our being (mental, emotional, and physical). It exposes our frailty and disturbs our spirit, soul, and body. Though we are tripartite beings, whatever affects one part of the body takes a toll on the other parts. When suffering persists, it calls for our attention, one way or another. Follow the story of Job in the next chapter.

Chapter Two: God is Getting Your Attention

Satan is the source of all evil and destruction. He is the chief agent of all our suffering. Jesus says in John 10:10a, *"The thief comes only to steal and kill and destroy."* The big question is: Why did God allow him to come in the first place? Everything that God allows has an eternal purpose.

In John 14:30–31, speaking of the devil, the Lord Jesus explains why the devil was allowed to come into the world—so that the world (that, of course, includes you and me) may learn that Jesus loves the Father and does exactly what the Father commands. If Satan hadn't been cast down into the earth, there would have been no suffering or destruction of any kind. Sin upon the earth would have been a non-issue. Adam and Eve wouldn't have been tempted, and the evil intent of man would have never been realized. There would have been no need for Jesus to come to earth to die for mankind. There wouldn't have been a clear picture of perfection, of sin and its wages, of God's love, or of His redemption through His Son, Jesus Christ.

Jesus's birth, His sacrificial life, and His resurrection and ascension demonstrated His love, submission, and obedience to the Father. Satan's coming provided an opportunity for us to see the manifested Son of God at work. The power that was afforded to him was given by the first man, Adam. Mankind, not Satan, was originally given dominion over the earth (Genesis 1:28); however, his fall from grace provided the great opportunity to learn of Jesus and His love, not only for His Father, but also for us. Jesus died in obedience to His Father to save us, so in one act, He demonstrated to the entire world His love for His Father and for mankind.

Hardship, difficulties, and sufferings in our lives have the potential to allow us to experience the full extent of God's love and grace. They can "break us or make us," depending on how we choose to respond.

Christ's love allows for an eternal exchange—grace for sin, healing for sickness and disease, deliverance for bondage, wealth and riches for poverty, knowledge and revelation for ignorance, light for darkness, and resurrection for death. Whatever the devil has stolen from us, God has restored through our Lord Jesus Christ. The wages of sin with all its

suffering and even death can now give way to the precious gift of God's eternal life through Jesus Christ. Has your sin left a crimson stain on you? Jesus's blood washes as white as snow. Recall that Jesus paid it all already. What a tremendous price to pay for our sins because of His amazing love for us as well as for His Father. God is interested in drawing our attention to His dominion life over suffering, sin, and even death. This was the case for many believers in the Bible who suffered, and so it is for us. Let's examine God's work in the life of a believer who suffered, and see what we can learn from his experience.

JOB'S EXPERIENCE

His Suffering

Consider the greatest Bible story of suffering and restoration. Many of us are either aware of, or familiar with, the story of Job. The first chapter of Job reveals that he was a rich and righteous man who feared God. He was so concerned about remaining upright, that whenever his sons had feasts at their homes to which his daughters were invited, he would afterwards sacrifice burnt offerings to God, in the event his children had sinned. The Lord Himself spoke of Job as a righteous man when He asked Satan if he had considered him (Job). This is when things began to change for Job, as the Lord removed the hedge placed around him and allowed Satan to afflict him. Over a short period of time, Job's life appeared to take a turn for the worse. His children died and he lost his property and his servants.

In Job 2:7–10, Job's condition further deteriorated to the extent that he was covered head to toe with painful sores. His wife was so devastated, she told him to curse God and die. His friends wept aloud when they saw him, tore their clothes, put dust on their heads, and sat on the ground with him for seven days and nights. So severe was Job's pain and distress, he lamented about the miseries of life and pondered on finding relief in death: Consider his words:

> "Why is light given to those in misery, and life to the bitter of soul, to those who long for death that does not come, who search for it more than for hidden treasure, who are filled with gladness and rejoice when they reach the grave? Why is life given to a man whose way is hidden, whom God has hedged in? For sighing has become my daily food; my groans pour out like water. What I feared has come upon me; I have no peace, no quietness; I have no rest, but only turmoil." Job 3:20–26

Maybe you're at a point where you, like Job, are crying out for relief from suffering, pain, agony, and grief. You may be grappling for understanding of what you have experienced or are going through, and you may think the answer is in death. STOP! God wants to reveal more of His heart to you, more of what He is doing in your life, what He is taking you through, and where He wants you to be. God has a plan for you, and He is taking you on a journey. Come with me a little further, READ ON, and let's discover what the Holy Spirit is saying concerning your suffering.

His Accusers

As we follow Job's story through Chapters 4–31, we witness a discourse between him and three of his friends—Eliphaz, Bildad, and Zophar—who all believed he was suffering because of sin in his life. But Job thought otherwise, because he believed he was a righteous man (Job 32:1). He didn't understand why he was suffering and questioned the reason for his birth. Here are some of their words:

ELIPHAZ'S WORDS:

"Consider now: Who, being innocent, has ever perished? Where were the upright ever destroyed? As I have observed, those who plow evil and those who sow trouble reap it. At the breath of God they perish; at the blast of his anger they are no more." (Job 4:7–9)

"Can a mortal be more righteous than God? Can even a strong man be more pure than his Maker? If God places no trust in his servants, if he charges his angels with error, how much more those who live in houses of clay, whose foundations are in the dust, who are crushed more readily than a moth!" (Job 4:17–19)

Call if you will, but who will answer you? To which of the holy ones will you turn? Resentment kills a fool, and envy slays the simple. I myself have seen a fool taking root, but suddenly his house was cursed. His children are far from safety, crushed in court without a defender. (Job 5:1–4)

For hardship does not spring from the soil, nor does trouble sprout from the ground. Yet man is born to trouble as surely as sparks fly upward. But if it were I, I would appeal to God; I would lay my cause before him. (Job 5:6–8)

Blessed is the man whom God corrects; so do not despise the discipline of the Almighty. For he wounds, but he also binds up; he injures, but his hands also heal." (Job 5:17–18)

JOB'S RESPONSE:

"Teach me, and I will be quiet; show me where I have been wrong. How painful are honest words! But what do your arguments prove? Do you mean to correct what I say, and treat the words of a despairing man as wind?"

(Job 6:24–26)

Relent, do not be unjust; reconsider, for my integrity is at stake. Is there any wickedness on my lips? Can my mouth not discern malice?" (Job 6:29–30)

"… I will speak out in the anguish of my spirit, I will complain in the bitterness of my soul." (Job 7:11b)

"What is mankind that you make so much of them, that you give them so much attention, that you examine them every morning and test them every moment? Will you never look away from me, or let me alone even for an instant? If I have sinned, what have I done to you, you who see everything we do? Why have you made me your target? Have I become a burden to you? Why do you not pardon my offenses and forgive my sins? For I will soon lie down in the dust; you will search for me, but I will be no more." (Job 7:17–21)

We will return to these words later.

BILDAD'S WORDS:

"How long will you say such things? Your words are a blustering wind. Does God pervert justice? Does the Almighty pervert what is right? When your children sinned against him, he gave them over to the penalty of their sin. But if you will seek God earnestly and plead with the Almighty, if you are pure and upright, even now he will rouse himself on your behalf and restore you to your prosperous place." (Job 8:2–6)

JOB'S RESPONSE:

"Although I am blameless, I have no concern for myself; I despise my own life. It is all the same; that is why I say, "He destroys both the blameless and the wicked." (Job 9:21–22)

"I loathe my very life; therefore I will give free rein to my complaint and speak out in the bitterness of my soul. I will say to God: Do not declare me guilty, but tell me what charges you have against me. Does it please you to oppress me, to spurn the work of your hands, while you smile on the plans of the wicked? Do you have eyes of flesh? Do you see as a mortal sees? Are your days like those of a mortal or your years like those of a strong man, that you must search out my faults and probe after my sin—though you know that I am not guilty and that no one can rescue me from your hand?" (Job 10:1–7)

"You gave me life and showed me kindness, and in your providence watched over my spirit. But this is what you concealed in your heart, and I know that this was in your mind: If I sinned, you would be watching me and would not let my offense go unpunished. If I am guilty—woe to me! Even if I am innocent, I cannot lift my head, for I am full of shame and drowned in my affliction. If I hold my head high, you stalk me like a lion and again display your awesome power against me. You bring new witnesses against me and increase your anger toward me; your forces come against me wave upon wave. Why then did you bring me out of the womb? I wish I had died before any eye saw me." (Job 10:12–18)

ZOPHAR'S WORDS:

"Are all these words to go unanswered? Is this talker to be vindicated? Will your idle talk reduce others to silence?

Will no one rebuke you when you mock? You say to God, "My beliefs are flawless and I am pure in your sight." Oh, how I wish that God would speak, that he would open his lips against you and disclose to you the secrets of wisdom, for true wisdom has two sides. Know this: God has even forgotten some of your sin." (Job 11:2–6)

"Yet if you devote your heart to Him and stretch out your hands to Him, if you put away the sin that is in your hand and allow no evil to dwell in your tent, then, free of fault, you will lift up your face; you will stand firm and without fear. You will surely forget your trouble, recalling it only as waters gone by." (Job 11:13–16)

JOB'S RESPONSE:

"My eyes have seen all this, my ears have heard and understood it. What you know, I also know; I am not inferior to you. But I desire to speak to the Almighty and to argue my case with God. You, however, smear me with lies; you are worthless physicians, all of you! If only you would be altogether silent! For you, that would be wisdom." (Job 13:1–5)

"Let God weigh me in honest scales and he will know that I am blameless—if my steps have turned from the path, if my heart has been led by my eyes, or if my hands have been defiled, then may others eat what I have sown, and may my crops be uprooted." (Job 31:6–8)

A fourth friend, Elihu, responded to the discourse in Chapters 32 to 37, and in Chapter 38, the Lord God Himself spoke. Here are some invaluable lessons about suffering that we can learn from their responses (below) to Job.

ELIHU'S RESPONSE:

In Job 32:4–5, 12, we see that Elihu, as the youngest of the four friends, waited respectfully before he spoke. When he heard what the three older men had to say, he was upset with them because he felt they had condemned Job without presenting strong arguments for doing so, arguments that would enlighten Job about the reason for his suffering (Job 32:12).

Let's consider some of the points Elihu raised to better understand why people suffer.

First, Elihu explained that God speaks in many different ways, such as through dreams, visions, an audible voice, or by chastening us through pain and suffering (Job 33:19–22).

Second, he pointed out that the "bed of affliction," and even the messengers of death, serve to get our attention. Otherwise, many of us wouldn't even pause momentarily to consider what God has to say to us about our life. Our pain and suffering provide opportunity for us to turn to God Almighty, the only one who can enlighten us and truly save us (Job 33:30). Our situation allows for us to surrender to God.

Third, our suffering challenges us to change our perspectives. We have to reckon with God, who is just. Whatever God allows happens to us for good reasons. He does not do evil (Job 34:10). Job's questioning of God was based on his ignorance of God and what God was doing in his life. We all need to ask these questions periodically. But remember, God's judgment is always righteous (Job 34:11–12; Isaiah 33:5; 2 Timothy 4:8). God Almighty is always righteous (Psalm 11:7, 145:17).

Fourth, God knows us very well, and He intends to make us better. He knows what's in our heart and can see our every move (Job 34:21). He sees within us the things to which we are blinded. How we respond to God's correction can allow for a worsening of our situations. Sometimes out of such ignorance, we question God's justice and integrity. Sometimes we speak in vain without any justification for the position we have taken on the matter. Many have refused even to repent and, as a result, have prolonged their own suffering. Job spoke without understanding (Job 34:35–37, 35:16).

As we suffer, we must understand God's perspective. Is there something He wants us to learn? He is the best teacher (Job 36:2–4, 22). Elihu acknowledged God's awesome wonder as the Creator who knows what He is doing and is in supreme control. He declared His sovereignty and described Him as excellent in power and the righteous judge of all. Even the wise people of this world are no match for God Almighty.

It is stated in Job 37:14–24 (KJV):

"Hearken unto this, O Job: stand still, and consider the wondrous works of God. Dost thou know when God disposed them, and caused the light of his cloud to shine? Dost thou know the balancings of the clouds, the wondrous works of him which is perfect in knowledge? How thy garments are warm, when he quieteth the earth by the south wind? Hast thou with him spread out the sky, which is strong, and as a molten looking glass? Teach us what we shall say unto him; for we cannot order our speech by reason of darkness. Shall it be told him that I speak? if a man speak, surely he shall be swallowed up. And now men see not the bright light which is in the clouds: but the wind passeth, and cleanseth them. Fair weather cometh out of the north: with God is terrible majesty. Touching the Almighty, we cannot find him out: he is excellent in power, and in judgment, and in plenty of justice: he will not afflict. Men do therefore fear him: he respecteth not any that are wise of heart."

Immediately following this declaration of who God is, God Himself speaks. In the next chapter, we'll consider God's response to all that was said.

Chapter Three: God Will Speak to You in Your Time of Suffering

In Job 38, God began to speak to Job and his friends. God neither condemned Job nor gave him a lecture about what he did right or wrong. Rather, He picked up from where Elihu stopped and responded to Job in the form of questions—questions that we too must ask ourselves as we face trials, afflictions, and suffering. Listen to His first words to Job: "*Who is this that obscures my plans with words without knowledge? Brace yourself like a man: I will question you and you shall answer me*" (Job 38:2–3 NIV).

> "Where were you when I laid the earth's foundation? Tell me, if you understand. Who marked off its dimensions? Surely you know! Who stretched a measuring line across it? On what were its footings set, or who laid its cornerstone—While the morning stars sang together and all the angels shouted for joy?" (Job 38:4–7 NIV)

Lesson 1: No matter what we're going through when we approach God, we must remember that *He is our Creator*. He has the blueprint of creation, and He established its foundation to the wonderment of all the angels who looked on. He therefore knows us and the world we live in, inside out. All other lessons are predicated on this understanding of who God is.

> "Who shut up the sea behind doors when it burst forth from the womb, when I made the clouds its garment and wrapped it in thick darkness, when I fixed limits for it and

set its doors and bars in place, when I said, "This far you may come and no farther; here is where your proud waves halt"?" (Job 38:8–11NIV)

Lesson 2: *God knows about boundaries and limits*. He established and understands the forces of nature. Consider the power of the seas that can overturn and destroy huge vessels, and tsunamis that send waves miles inland. God knows the huge pressure that lies within the seas, and He is the one who sets its boundaries. Even when it rains, He determines how much we get. The Creator, God Almighty, knows just how much pressure we can manage. **He sets our limits**.

> "Have you ever given orders to the morning, or shown the dawn its place, that it might take the earth by the edges and shake the wicked out of it? The earth takes shape like clay under a seal; its features stand out like those of a garment. The wicked are denied their light, and their upraised arm is broken." (Job 38:12–15NIV)

Lesson 3: *God has authority and dominion over all things*. He gave the order for things to come into being. He formed land by speaking it into being and separated night from day. He exposes the wicked and disarms them. It is who God is and what He does!

In like manner, when God placed Adam and Eve in the Garden of Eden, He made us in His image and gave us the authority to rule over all things on earth … to have dominion (Genesis 1:26). We had the responsibility to take our rightful place and keep things in order. But then the sin of Adam and Eve led to the loss of that authority. Jesus Christ's death on the cross, His resurrection from the dead, and ascension to God the Father allowed us to regain that authority and dominion. ***When we are born again through faith in Jesus Christ, we possess the authority to exercise that dominion*** and put things back in order. Jesus Christ said to His disciples in Luke 10:19: "*I have given you authority to trample on snakes and scorpions and to overcome all the power of the enemy; nothing will harm you.*" Also, the Apostle Paul wrote to the church in Ephesus:

"I pray that the eyes of your heart may be enlightened in order that you may know the hope to which he has called you, the riches of his glorious inheritance in his holy people, and his incomparably great power for us who believe. That power is the same as the mighty strength he exerted when he raised Christ from the dead and seated him at his right hand in the heavenly realms, far above all rule and authority, power and dominion, and every name that is invoked, not only in the present age but also in the one to come. And God placed all things under his feet and appointed him to be head over everything for the church, which is his body, the fullness of him who fills everything in every way." (Ephesians 1:18–23).

The coming of Jesus Christ, the Son of God, the shedding of His blood and death on Calvary's cross, and His resurrection, placed dominion and authority back into the hands of believers. In accordance with the Word of God, we can now take authority over sickness, afflictions, trials and tribulations, speak to them in the name of Jesus, and see God's power work in such situations.

How aware are we of the power and dominion that God has given us? Have we been in the right relationship with God so that we can hear and understand what He says about our afflictions, trials, and tribulations? Do we exercise the faith to activate that power for healing or deliverance? The children of God are endowed with the power to reorder things that are out of order, to take authority in denying "the light of the wicked" and breaking their upraised arms, as stated in Job 38:15.

Lesson 4: God will guide, strengthen and shine His light on our situation.

"Have you journeyed to the springs of the sea or walked in the recesses of the deep? Have the gates of death been shown to you? Have you seen the gates of the deepest darkness? Have you comprehended the vast expanses of the earth? Tell me, if you know all this.

What is the way to the abode of light? And where does darkness reside? Can you take them to their places? Do you know the paths to their dwellings? Surely you know, for you were already born! You have lived so many years!" (Job 38:16–21)

God has covered the highest heights and deepest depths. He knows the origin of light and darkness, and He knows wherever they are present in the world, in nations, in families, in places of worship, and in our individual lives. God knows where you are and what you face. That's why God says in His Word, through King David, *"Even though I walk through the darkest valley, I will fear no evil, for you are with me; your rod and your staff, they comfort me. You prepare a table before me in the presence of my enemies"* (Psalm 23: 4–5a). Again, God says in Psalm 139:1–12:

"You have searched me, Lord, and you know me. You know when I sit and when I rise; you perceive my thoughts from afar. You discern my going out and my lying down; you are familiar with all my ways. Before a word is on my tongue you, Lord, know it completely. You hem me in behind and before, and you lay your hand upon me. Such knowledge is too wonderful for me, too lofty for me to attain. Where can I go from your Spirit? Where can I flee from your presence? If I go up to the heavens, you are there; if I make my bed in the depths, you are there. If I rise on the wings of the dawn, if I settle on the far side of the sea, even there your hand will guide me, your right hand will hold me fast. If I say, Surely the darkness will hide me and the light become night around me, even the darkness will not be dark to you; the night will shine like the day, for darkness is as light to you."

Wherever we are, whatever the suffering or sorrow we face—be it affliction, sickness, death of loved ones, tribulations and trials, *God is right there with us to guide, hold fast, strengthen, and shine His light in us and on our situation.*

Lesson 5: God is the Waymaker

> "Have you entered the storehouses of the snow or seen the storehouses of the hail, which I reserve for times of trouble, for days of war and battle? What is the way to the place where the lightning is dispersed, or the place where the east winds are scattered over the earth? Who cuts a channel for the torrents of rain, and a path for the thunderstorm, to water a land where no one lives, an uninhabited desert, to satisfy a desolate wasteland and make it sprout with grass? Does the rain have a father? Who fathers the drops of dew? From whose womb comes the ice? Who gives birth to the frost from the heavens when the waters become hard as stone, when the surface of the deep is frozen?" (Job 38:22–30)

God has a way through every challenge. **He is the Waymaker**. As the Way maker, He uses even nature to deal with times of trouble (Exodus 9:19, 23; Psalms 18:12–14). He determines the pathway for nature to water deserts and wastelands, and to change the state of liquid water to ice. In like manner, God will make a way for us as we face our difficulties. Listen to what He said to the Israelites in Isaiah 43:18–19: "*Forget the former things; do not dwell on the past. See, I am doing a new thing! Now it springs up; do you not perceive it? I am making a way in the wilderness and streams in the wasteland.*"

Today, we have access to the same Way maker, God Almighty. The originator of the dew and ice has the amazing power to freeze "*the surface of the deep.*" The Word of God says in 1st Timothy 2:5: "*For there is one God and one mediator between God and mankind, the man Christ Jesus.*" Jesus Himself said in John 14:6: "*I am the way and the truth and the life. No one comes to the Father except through me.*" We can't find the way on our own; we must believe and trust in Jesus, our Creator, the almighty and omniscient one, through every challenge we face.

Lesson 6: God is the Almighty. He is able to provide whatever is necessary and appropriate for each season.

"Can you bind the chains of the Pleiades? Can you loosen Orion's belt? Can you bring forth the constellations in their seasons or lead out the Bear with its cubs? Do you know the laws of the heavens? Can you set up God's dominion over the earth?" (Job 38:31–33)

"Can you raise your voice to the clouds and cover yourself with a flood of water? Do you send the lightning bolts on their way? Do they report to you, "Here we are"? Who gives the ibis wisdom or gives the rooster understanding? Who has the wisdom to count the clouds? Who can tip over the water jars of the heavens when the dust becomes hard and the clods of earth stick together?" (Job 38:34–38)

God again confronted Job with questions that relate to His awesome wonder. He invited Job to consider the constellations in the heavens, and the clusters of stars that form patterns in the night sky. Astrologers note that these constellations have been appearing every year at the same time for thousands of years. God Almighty binds these stars together, and only He has the power to loosen them. He establishes the laws of the heavens so that these stars appear in specific seasons.

His control over the heavens is also seen in His authority to speak to the clouds to give rain and to send lightning. We also see reference to the wisdom and understanding that are seen in creatures made by God. Storks, for example, can be timekeepers, whose early morning crowing can serve as a wakeup call and whose screeches warn of danger. God has dominion over the heavens and the earth.

The God of heaven and earth is the Creator. He is all powerful. He has power over all things that concern us. He understands and controls the times and seasons we go through in life. Sometimes life appears warm, bright, and fruitful; other times, like the autumn, we go through shedding, when we lose or are forced to release people, places, or things in life. Winter times see us battered by experiences that may be cold and hostile, or that present a mix of sunshine and cold. Finally, during spring times of relief and reprieve, when harsh conditions break, we feel as if we're recovering.

We begin to plant seeds of hope and life in anticipation of reaping rich rewards. He, **God Almighty, is able to provide whatever is necessary and appropriate for each season.**

> "Do you hunt the prey for the lioness and satisfy the hunger of the lions when they crouch in their dens or lie in wait in a thicket? Who provides food for the raven when its young cry out to God and wander about for lack of food?" (Job 38:39–41)

Here again, Job is directed to consider that God is the great provider. We too must remember that God cares and is able to provide for us.

Lesson 7: God makes everything beautiful in His time.

> "Do you know when the mountain goats give birth? Do you watch when the doe bears her fawn? Do you count the months till they bear? Do you know the time they give birth? They crouch down and bring forth their young; their labor pains are ended. Their young thrive and grow strong in the wilds; they leave and do not return. Who let the wild donkey go free? Who untied its ropes? I gave it the wasteland as its home, the salt flats as its habitat. It laughs at the commotion in the town; it does not hear a driver's shout. It ranges the hills for its pasture and searches for any green thing. Will the wild ox consent to serve you? Will it stay by your manger at night? Can you hold it to the furrow with a harness? Will it till the valleys behind you? Will you rely on it for its great strength? Will you leave your heavy work to it? Can you trust it to haul in your grain and bring it to your threshing floor? The wings of the ostrich flap joyfully, though they cannot compare with the wings and feathers of the stork. She lays her eggs on the ground and lets them warm in the sand, unmindful that a foot may crush them, that some wild animal may trample them. She treats her young harshly, as if they were not hers; she cares not that her labor was in vain, for

God did not endow her with wisdom or give her a share of good sense. Yet when she spreads her feathers to run, she laughs at horse and rider. Do you give the horse its strength or clothe its neck with a flowing mane? Do you make it leap like a locust, striking terror with its proud snorting? It paws fiercely, rejoicing in its strength, and charges into the fray. It laughs at fear, afraid of nothing; it does not shy away from the sword. The quiver rattles against its side, along with the flashing spear and lance. In frenzied excitement it eats up the ground; it cannot stand still when the trumpet sounds. At the blast of the trumpet it snorts, "Aha!" It catches the scent of battle from afar, the shout of commanders and the battle cry. Does the hawk take flight by your wisdom and spread its wings toward the south? Does the eagle soar at your command and build its nest on high? It dwells on a cliff and stays there at night; a rocky crag is its stronghold. From there it looks for food; its eyes detect it from afar. Its young ones feast on blood, and where the slain are, there it is." (Job 39:1–30)

Job was challenged to once again consider God's awesome power and wonder as it's displayed in the creatures He created. God asked Job to consider His reproductive power (Job 39:1–4), His liberating power (Job 39:5–18), and His power to give strength and tenacity (Job 39:18–38). If He does all these for animals that were not made in His image, what wonders will He do for us who were made in His image (see Genesis 1:27), and for whom, out of abundant love, He sent His Son, Jesus Christ to die (John 3:16)? Do you need a resurgence of life in your body, in your family, in your walk with God, and in your finances? Do you need strength and tenacity to press through the challenges you face? Look to God, your Creator. Commit your life and your situation to Him and trust Him to work in you whatever resources you need and what is best for you in this season. No matter what it is, God, who never lies, says in His Word that we will face challenges as we go from one season to another, and we cannot comprehend it all, but He makes everything beautiful in **its time** and **season** (Ecclesiastes 3:1, 10–11).

But that was not the end of God's response to Job and his friends. God knows our heart and He hears the whispers of lingering thoughts that say: "If you are all that, the Great Almighty God who knows all things, then why, God? How could you do this to me?" Let's continue to search the Word of God to hear how He answered this question.

Chapter Four: Why, God? This Is Unfair!

For those who might be saying: "God, how could you do this to me? This is unfair. You're not a just God! You say you love me, yet you allow me to hurt so much." God's response to Job will provide an answer. God Almighty invited Job into conversation to correct Him. The Lord said to Job: "*Will the one who contends with the Almighty correct him? Let him who accuses God answer him!*" (Job 40:2)

At this point, Job realizes that He is out of his league. In Job 40:3–5, he responds with brokenness and penitence: "*Then Job answered the Lord: 'I am unworthy—how can I reply to you? I put my hand over my mouth. I spoke once, but I have no answer— twice, but I will say no more.'*"

The questions continue, and we include the words of God in this book to encourage you, like Job, to consider these questions.

Lesson 8: God is the Omnipotent (all powerful) and Omniscient (all knowing) One. Our unwavering trust in God will cause our latter end to be greater than the former.

> "Then the Lord spoke to Job out of the storm: Brace yourself like a man; I will question you, and you shall answer me. Would you discredit my justice? Would you condemn me to justify yourself? Do you have an arm like God's, and can your voice thunder like his? Then adorn yourself with glory and splendor, and clothe yourself in honor and majesty. Unleash the fury of your wrath, look at all who

are proud and bring them low, look at all who are proud
and humble them, crush the wicked where they stand.
Bury them all in the dust together; shroud their faces in
the grave. Then I myself will admit to you that your own
right hand can save you." (Job 40:6–14)

Job had lost his possessions. His sheep, oxen, camels, servants, and his sons
and daughters were all killed in one night (Job 1:13–18). In addition, he
had been afflicted with painful sores all over his body, so even his friends
were shocked at his appearance (Job 2:7–8, 11–13; 6:14–15;12:4). Job fell
into the pit of despair, describing the weight of his anguish and misery as
more than the weight of *"the sand of the seas"* (Job 6:3). Altogether, he had
lost family, fortune, fame and friends. We can well appreciate his despair,
the internal conflicts he faced as he considered his physical, mental, and
emotional state; the uncertainties about how to respond to all that had
happened to him; the questions about God, who says He hears us and loves
us; questions about his commitment and service to God over the years;
questions about God's goodness; and questions about his own fate.

In spite of this, Job refused to curse God, as suggested by his wife. He was
resolute in holding fast to his faith in God, though he felt he was denied
justice (Job 27:1–2).

Maybe you've been there, or maybe that's where you are now. The questions are troubling. "Why, God?" "Why me, Lord?" "Where did I go
wrong?" "How could you do this to me?" "What about your promises on
hearing the cries of your people, about saving, healing, and delivering your
people?" "Where is your mercy?" "Haven't I been faithful to you?" Maybe
you're at the point where you're even bitter toward God. Stay with us a little
longer as we continue to hear what God says and wrestle with His revelation about suffering.

"Look at Behemoth, which I made along with you and
which feeds on grass like an ox. What strength it has in its
loins, what power in the muscles of its belly! Its tail sways
like a cedar; the sinews of its thighs are close-knit. Its bones
are tubes of bronze, its limbs like rods of iron. It ranks first

30

among the works of God, yet its Maker can approach it with his sword. The hills bring it their produce, and all the wild animals play nearby. Under the lotus plants it lies, hidden among the reeds in the marsh. The lotuses conceal it in their shadow; the poplars by the stream surround it. A raging river does not alarm it; it is secure, though the Jordan should surge against its mouth. Can anyone capture it by the eyes, or trap it and pierce its nose?" (Job 40:15–24)

"Can you pull in Leviathan with a fishhook or tie down its tongue with a rope? Can you put a cord through its nose or pierce its jaw with a hook? Will it keep begging you for mercy? Will it speak to you with gentle words? Will it make an agreement with you for you to take it as your slave for life? Can you make a pet of it like a bird or put it on a leash for the young women in your house? Will traders barter for it? Will they divide it up among the merchants? Can you fill its hide with harpoons or its head with fishing spears? If you lay a hand on it, you will remember the struggle and never do it again! Any hope of subduing it is false; the mere sight of it is overpowering. No one is fierce enough to rouse it. Who then is able to stand against me? Who has a claim against me that I must pay? Everything under heaven belongs to me. I will not fail to speak of Leviathan's limbs, its strength and its graceful form. Who can strip off its outer coat? Who can penetrate its double coat of armor? Who dares open the doors of its mouth, ringed about with fearsome teeth? Its back has rows of shields tightly sealed together; each is so close to the next that no air can pass between. They are joined fast to one another; they cling together and cannot be parted. Its snorting throws out flashes of light; its eyes are like the rays of dawn. Flames stream from its mouth; sparks of fire shoot out. Smoke pours from its nostrils as from a boiling pot over burning reeds. Its breath sets coals ablaze, and flames dart from its mouth. Strength resides in its neck; dismay goes before it. The folds of its flesh are tightly joined; they are firm and immovable. Its chest is hard as rock, hard as a lower millstone. When it rises up, the mighty are terrified; they retreat before its thrashing. The sword that reaches it has no effect, nor does the spear or the dart or the javelin. Iron it treats like straw and bronze like rotten wood. Arrows do not make it flee; slingstones are like chaff to it. A club seems to it but a piece of straw; it laughs at the rattling of the lance. Its undersides are jagged potsherds, leaving a trail in the mud like a threshing sledge. It makes the depths churn like a boiling caldron and stirs up the sea like a pot of ointment. It leaves a glistening wake behind it; one would think the deep had white hair. Nothing on earth is its equal—a creature without fear. It looks down on all that are haughty; it is king over all that are proud." (Job 41:1–34)

We must consider a central point in these words from the Lord: God is the omnipotent (all powerful), omniscient (all knowing) one. In His wisdom, He made two awesome creatures, Behemoth and Leviathan that were strong and powerful. Of Behemoth, God says, "*It ranks first among the works of God, yet its Maker can approach it with his sword*" (Isaiah 40:19). Concerning Leviathan, God said "*Nothing on earth is its equal—a creature without fear. It looks down on all that are haughty; it is king over all that are proud*" (Job 41:33–34).

God made them, and He has the power to take them out. In like manner, God, the Creator and Maker, has the power to humble every proud person. The wicked are no match for Him, because the power of life and death is in His hands.

But the Almighty is also all knowing. His wisdom is reflected in His created world and all that is in it, all that was so perfectly designed in beauty and with the power to feed and sustain itself, even in the deserts. His wisdom is seen in the detailed description of the fierceness of the artistry and fortitude of Behemoth and Leviathan that make them indomitable creatures.

The Scripture says in Jeremiah 10:12 (KJV): *"He hath made the earth by his power, he hath established the world by his wisdom, and hath stretched out the heavens by his discretion."* If you think we can outmatch God in wisdom, read 1 Corinthians 1:19–20, 27 (KJV):

> "For it is written, I will destroy the wisdom of the wise, and will bring to nothing the understanding of the prudent. Where is the wise? Where is the scribe? Where is the disputer of this world? hath not God made foolish the wisdom of this world? … But God hath chosen the foolish things of the world to confound the wise; and God hath chosen the weak things of the world to confound the things which are mighty."

Let's consider Job's response to God.

> "Then Job replied to the Lord: "I know that you can do all things; no purpose of yours can be thwarted. You asked, 'Who is this that obscures my plans without knowledge?' Surely I spoke of things I did not understand, things too wonderful for me to know. You said, 'Listen now, and I will speak; I will question you, and you shall answer me.' My ears had heard of you but now my eyes have seen you. Therefore I despise myself and repent in dust and ashes." (Job 42:1–6)

Job had grasped God's words and had come to better understand His ways. God is omnipotent. He can do all things, but He is also omniscient, so whatever He does is wrapped up in His wise purpose. It's never without good reason, and His purpose always extends beyond us, because He is God of all creation. Out of his experience of suffering, Job's understanding of God expanded and his attitude changed. His friends' understanding and attitude also expanded and changed, and our understanding and attitudes are also being transformed as we follow Job's story.

Job became broken and penitent, and his three friends also had to repent:

"And it was so, that after the Lord had spoken these words unto Job, the Lord said to Eliphaz the Temanite, My wrath is kindled against thee, and against thy two friends: for ye have not spoken of me the thing that is right, as my servant Job hath. Therefore take unto you now seven bullocks and seven rams, and go to my servant Job, and offer up for yourselves a burnt offering; and my servant Job shall pray for you: for him will I accept: lest I deal with you after your folly, in that ye have not spoken of me the thing which is right, like my servant Job. So Eliphaz the Temanite and Bildad the Shuhite and Zophar the Naamathite went, and did according as the Lord commanded them: the Lord also accepted Job." (Job 42:7–9, KJV)

God didn't leave Job in his suffering. Job finished in a better position spiritually, mentally, emotionally, and physically.

Job's story continues in Job 42:10–17 (KJV):

"And the Lord turned the captivity of Job, when he prayed for his friends: also the Lord gave Job twice as much as he had before. Then came there unto him all his brethren, and all his sisters, and all they that had been of his acquaintance before, and did eat bread with him in his house: and they bemoaned him, and comforted him over all the evil that the Lord had brought upon him: every man also gave him a piece of money, and every one an earring of gold. So the Lord blessed the latter end of Job more than his beginning: for he had fourteen thousand sheep, and six thousand camels, and a thousand yoke of oxen, and a thousand she asses. He had also seven sons and three daughters. And he called the name of the first, Jemima; and the name of the second, Kezia; and the name of the third, Kerenhappuch. And in all the land were no women found so fair as the daughters of Job: and their father gave them inheritance among their brethren. After this lived Job an hundred and forty years, and saw his sons, and his sons' sons, even four generations. So Job died, being old and full of days."

Has God gotten your attention? What was He doing to Job?

The Word of God says in Romans 12:1–2 (KJV):

> "… Present your bodies a living sacrifice, holy, acceptable unto God, which is your reasonable service. And be not conformed to this world: but be ye transformed by the renewing of your mind, that ye may prove what is that good, and acceptable, and perfect, will of God."

Job's suffering and afflictions gave him experiential knowledge of God that propelled him to a greater level of surrender to God. At this level, there is less of the sinful nature and greater intimacy with God and His divine nature.

What was God doing to Job? God judges or chastens us towards our redemption, not condemnation. He desires to save us from eternal damnation. God desires that we not be judged with the judgment meant for the wicked. We must beware of turning to evil as we endure hardship, suffering, or even chastising of the Lord. Remember how Cain killed his brother, Abel, because he did not take heed to God's warning? We must choose affliction rather than iniquity.

It's important to heed the warnings of God and learn from our mistakes, or else we'll perish by the sword without knowledge. Those who don't forgive, who don't seek God's forgiveness, or have no godly sorrow that leads to repentance will continue in their sin, and their situations will take them deeper into the pits. Godly sorrow leads to true repentance. A broken and contrite heart God will not despise. Take the time to read and consider what happened to Eli's priestly household (1 Samuel 3: 11–19) and David's cry of repentance in Psalm 51.

God will teach us in our afflictions. What lessons do we have to learn? We learn nothing good if we turn away from God and choose iniquity. We must know God in our afflictions and remember who He is at all times. God's judgment is first unto redemption, but turning away from Him will ultimately lead to eternal damnation.

God is almighty and excellent in power and judgment. He's the most righteous judge of all. His work in creation demonstrates His knowledge of boundaries. He laid the foundations of the earth and set limits and boundaries for all of creation. God brings alignment to the entire universe.

God gave us the opportunity to manage the earth with Him by giving us the dominion mandate through our Lord Jesus Christ (1 Corinthians 3:9). Jesus demonstrated His power of authority on earth. We too must take our rightful place and realign things that have been out of alignment in our lives.

We must also exercise our faith in times of suffering, knowing that God will see us through. He knows how much we can bear in our suffering and tribulations, and He won't give us more than we can bear (1 Corinthians 10:13). We have the authority through Christ to speak to situations in our lives, to bind and loose. God is our great deliverer. We must call upon Him in times of need. All things are under His control. All power is subject to God. Humble yourself before Him, and He will exalt you in due time. Be broken before Him, and He will not despise or turn you away. Be penitent before God. God elevates those deserving of elevation and humbles those who need humility. The power of life and death is in His hand. He has power over all of His creation. Job finally confessed that he knew that God can do all things and that no plan of God can be thwarted. The ultimate conclusion for Job was to be broken and repent before God. As a result of his new-found understanding of God in his suffering and his change of attitude before God, his latter life was greater than the former. Evidently, God designed the evil he endured for his good.

We must continuously remind ourselves of the purpose of life. We're not simply called to happiness or to health, but to holiness. Our soul prospers in that environment (3 John 1:2). Too many of our desires and interests digress from God's perfect will for our lives. James writes that we desire to have but do not have because we do not ask God. When we ask, we do not receive, because we ask with wrong motives to satisfy our worldly pleasures (James 4:2–3).

"Many of them may be right, noble and good, and may later be fulfilled, but in the meantime, God must cause their importance to us to decrease. The only thing that truly matters is whether a person will accept the God who will make him holy. At all costs, a person must have the right relationship with God." – By Oswald Chambers[1].

God is interested in the more eternal things of life. Whatever we go through in this life is only momentary. God will use it to work in us the more eternal things.

He desires for us to focus not on the temporary, but on the eternal. Stay with me as we consider more earnestly kingdom living and suffering.

---

1   Oswald Chambers, My Utmost for His Highest, (Dodd Mead &Co.), 1935

Chapter Five:
Understanding Kingdom
Living and Suffering

(The Significance of) Righteousness,
Peace, and Joy in the Holy Ghost.

The Word of God says:

> "For the kingdom of God is not a matter o`f eating and
> drinking, but of righteousness, peace and joy in the
> Holy Spirit, because anyone who serves Christ in this
> way is pleasing to God and receives human approval"
> (Romans 14:17–18).

But what does this have to do with suffering?

To be at war with Satan is not synonymous with having righteousness, peace, or joy in the Holy Ghost. We can be at war but not be in right standing with God. We can be at war but not have the joy of the Lord. Not understanding this can be self-defeating, nonproductive, and harmful. Many are killed in war with Satan because of such a fallacy.

What then is the significance of righteousness in the Holy Ghost? Righteousness is instilled in us when we surrender our lives to God (2 Corinthians 5:21). This means that we need to be in alignment with who we are in Christ. Our prayers must focus on having the right relationship with our Creator. Our righteousness must surpass the righteousness of the Pharisees. God cares about us having the right relationship with Him, without which we won't obey Him. Jesus learned obedience because of the things He suffered (Hebrews 5:8). Despite Job's righteous living, even he had to come to the realization that he wasn't faultless. He had to repent and realign himself with God.

Let's consider the significance of having the peace of God. As a young man, I was a member of a gang. One Sunday afternoon in the 1980s, at the height of political violence in my country, I was attacked by men who were members of an opposing gang. They beat me to the point of near death. That experience caused me to become very reflective. I began to examine the life I was living, a life filled with mental and physical turbulence in a neighborhood rife with political and gang violence that almost took my life. I needed a change, and I decided to surrender my life to God. What the enemy intended for evil, God turned around for good.

Satan wanted me dead, but God, in His sovereignty, said no. God allowed this attack for His own purpose, to redirect my life back to Him. I'd actually grown up in the church as a lad; however, like most teenagers, I departed and became wayward. I became involved in gang activities, drugs, and sexual promiscuity, which took me away from God's protection. God allowed this suffering in my life to gain my attention so that I would cry out to Him and be restored. Although I had lots of opportunities to get revenge, I thought otherwise, recognizing that God had a plan for my life. God knows how to chasten those He loves and bring back His lost sheep to the fold. I can't recall ever making a decision for the Lord as a child, but God in His infinite wisdom knows those who belong to Him. He knows all His sons and daughters. He has suffered to bring us back to Him through His own Son, Jesus Christ (Philippians 2:5–8).

God uses our need for peace (to satisfy our humanity) to compel our destiny into His kingdom. The extent of our peace depends on how well rooted we are in God Almighty and Jesus Christ, our Lord and Savior. It depends on how well we know Him and practice living like Him. That's why in the midst of the storm at sea, Jesus was sleeping (Matthew 8:23–27). When He was awakened by the disciples, He said:

"You of little faith, why are you so afraid?" Then he got up and rebuked the winds and the waves, and it was completely calm. The men were amazed and asked, "What kind of man is this? Even the winds and the waves obey him!" (Matthew 8:26–27)

He is the peace that we so desire in person—peace personified.

I'll share another personal experience to demonstrate the significance of peace in the kingdom. My family and I attended prayer meeting on Wednesday nights at the church we were attending. One night, the leader began praying for the peace of God to be upon somebody in the room. Since my family had just lost a dear friend, I thought the leader could be referring to me, that I may need God's peace. However, I didn't accept that the word of knowledge was for me.

That night, I couldn't fall asleep, and I didn't know why. I started to reflect on my friend who had died two days earlier. Then my right ear began to itch. I rubbed it so hard, it bled profusely. I tried everything to stop the bleeding, even while I was falling asleep. Then I realized that someone was looking in my ears, and I explained to the person how I'd caused it to bleed. I thought the person looking in my ears was my wife, but then I realized that she was asleep.

I forgot about the experience until the following afternoon. The Lord began to speak to me about the importance of His kingdom and the significance of righteousness, peace, and joy in His kingdom. He went on to explain that He cared about me and was the person who touched me and looked into my ear. He said that He caused the leader of the prayer group to pray for us to have peace because it was important for us, especially in times of distress. The encounter I had in the night was very comforting and caused me to experience God's peace. I was able to fall asleep soon after. Without God's peace, we are troubled on every side and will live defeated lives in all our relationships.

The kingdom of God brings righteousness, peace, and joy in the Holy Ghost. When we understand its significance in our prayer life—and in our whole life as children of God's kingdom—we'll be completely transformed.

We'll no longer pray amiss but rather within the will of God. Righteousness, peace, and joy in the Holy Ghost are at the heart of God.

Let's consider the joy of God. Our understanding of joy is also important for kingdom living. The Bible says the joy of the Lord is our strength, and that out of our *"belly shall flow rivers of living water"* (John 7:38, KJV). It is *"joy unspeakable and full of glory"* (1 Peter 1:8). We need God's great joy if we're to endure hardship and suffering. Jesus was only able to endure the cross because of the joy that was set before Him. There is joy enough for every one of us to have our own share of it. It is the joy of the Lord given to us that makes us strong (Hebrews 12:2; Nehemiah 8:10).God will allow us to experience hardship so we can be pruned like fruit trees, to become a people of righteousness, peace, and joy in the Holy Ghost. The next chapter speaks to this act of pruning.

Chapter Six: Drinking from the Cup of the Lord

"Beloved, think it not strange concerning the fiery trial which is to try you as though some strange things happened to you." (1 Peter 4:12 KJV),

When you enter in diverse temptation, it's the Father's way of disciplining and training you to become like His Son, Jesus Christ. This is a part of the pruning process. Your intimate relationship with Christ is pivotal in the transformation of your whole life and your ultimate position in the kingdom of God. What we do with our relationship with our Lord and Savior Jesus Christ will eventually determine how God uses us and our ultimate position (where we sit) in the kingdom.

Our willingness to partake of Christ's suffering, bear one another's burdens, be in travail, take up our own cross, and follow Jesus to the end determines how much we drink from His cup of suffering. Your willingness to lay down your life, to despise any shame for the sake of the cross, is an example of drinking from the cup of the Lord (1 Corinthians 10:21). The burdens we bear, the suffering we experience, and the cross we carry will vary. It may be physical, spiritual, mental, and/or emotional. For one person, it may be facing illness or death; for another, it may be coping with devastating relationships with family, friends, church members, or coworkers. For another, it may be facing a mental and/or emotional breakdown and seemingly inexplicable recurring setbacks or spiritual torment arising from association with witchcraft or demonic possession. It may be a personal struggle, or it may be related to family, friends, and associates at work, church, in the larger body of Christ, or in your nation. It reminds me of the theme of a Baptist church youth camp I attended: "The Cost of Christian Discipleship." It demands taking up the cross, but don't forget that Jesus triumphed in the resurrection.

We encounter Him in a personal way when we allow the living Word of God to become meat for our souls. We "eat" His flesh as we live by the Word of God through faith.

> *"Man shall not live by bread alone, but by every word that proceedeth out of the mouth of God"* (Matthew 4:4).

This analogy likens God's actions to a mother bird giving food to her chicks from her mouth. God feeds our souls as we receive from Him the living Word and encounter His very breath, the breath of life.

God's life-giving words reveal His personhood to us. We're better able to be transformed when we encounter Him in His Word. God is more interested in making us to be like His Son than anything else we might desire. He wants to manifest His glory through us. This can only be accomplished if we lay down our lives and are willing to take up our cross and follow Jesus. As we continue to travail in our suffering, we shed that which does not belong, and all that is left of us is Christ.

Jesus Christ lives in us, but His life will only be manifested as we surrender our life, as we die daily to sin and darkness and allow God to shine the light of His glory in our hearts and through us. The more we choose to die, the more of God's presence will be manifested in our lives:

> *"... unless a kernel of wheat falls to the ground and dies, it remains only a single seed. But if it dies, it produces many seeds."* (John 12:24).

God will position you to become a partaker of Christ's suffering by having you "drink from the cup of the Lord and eat of His flesh." His sweat that represents drops of blood must touch your life and mine, so that the anointing on His life might be poured out on us. Yokes will be broken and we will be delivered to lead lives that are most pleasing to God and reflective of His glory.

The Apostle Paul wrote:

> *"I have been crucified with Christ and I no longer live, but Christ lives in me. The life I live in the body, I live by faith in the Son of God, who loved me and gave Himself for me."* (Galatians 2:20).

Faith in God requires you to lay down your life, to die to self, to give Christ first place in your life and to have only Him living in you. The troubles and trials that we face are described by Paul in 2 Corinthians 4:17 as *"light and momentary troubles"* that achieve *"for us an eternal glory that far outweighs them all."* When you "drink from the cup of the Lord and eat of His flesh," you feed and live on the Word of God so that you will be able to do what Christ did, and even greater, because the Father is repositioning you to be like His Son.

Praise God, we are being changed *"from glory to glory"* (2 Corinthians 3:18, KJV). The glory of this latter house is incomparable to that of the former. Nothing can stop you when you submit your fleshly desires and allow the Word of God to become flesh in you. The next section speaks to the killing of our own fleshly desires.

Chapter Seven: Suffering Kills the Flesh

"For I know that in me (that is, in my flesh,) dwelleth no good thing: for to will is present with me; but how to perform that which is good I find not" (Romans 7:18, KJV).

In Exodus 16:1–27, the Bible speaks of a time when the children of Israel left Egypt and were wandering in the wilderness. They complained that Moses and Aaron had taken them out of Egypt into the desert to starve. God heard their grumblings and rained down manna from heaven to feed them, telling them exactly how much to take for each day. He wanted to test their obedience to Him. Some gathered too much, and some gathered a little. But when each was measured, they all had the same amount. Some Israelites tried to keep a portion for the next day, but in the morning, the manna was covered with maggots and had started to smell. God won't allow you to preserve the flesh and lose sight of Him, the Giver of Life. Rather, He requires that we seek Him more than anything else.

Jesus said in Matthew 6:33 (KJV): *"But seek ye first the kingdom of God, and his righteousness; and all these things shall be added unto you."* The way to the kingdom of God is through Jesus: *"For there is one God and one mediator between God and mankind, the man Christ Jesus"* (1 Timothy 2:5). Let's aim to be like Jesus. The Apostle Paul wrote:

> "I am crucified with Christ: nevertheless I live; yet not I, but Christ liveth in me: and the life which I now live in the flesh I live by the faith of the son of God, who loved me

and gave himself for me." (Galatians 2:20, KJV)

The flesh will profit nothing. For Christ to live and reign in your life, the flesh must be slain. The flesh must die to your ways and your understandings.

> *"My people are destroyed for lack of knowledge." (Hosea 4:6 KJV)*

There cannot be proper understanding without knowledge of the truth. Some are weak because they fail to understand. Some are wicked because they refuse to understand:

> "Understanding is a wellspring of life unto him that hath it: but the instruction of fools is folly" (Proverbs 16:22 KJV).

The key to being victorious in our sufferings is to have understanding:

> *"… with all thy getting, get understanding"* (Proverbs 4:7, KJV).

Understanding means knowing Jesus and emulating His life.

Don't be disturbed when the flesh shows up; it's just that old man demonstrating the old nature that's not fully dead. Kill it and bring your members under subjection to the Lordship of Christ. Don't get disappointed because you messed up again. Be glad, because that demon of the flesh showed up that it might be slain. Just don't leave it as is … *kill it.*

> *"Verily, verily I said unto you, Except a corn of wheat fall into the ground and die, it abideth alone: but if it die, it bringeth forth much fruit"* (John 12:24, KJV).

Do you want to see Christ manifest in you? Kill the flesh; let it be slain.

> *"Humble yourselves therefore under the mighty hand of God, that he may exalt you in due time"* (1 Peter 5:6, KJV).

Work at being humble. Pray, *Lord, teach me your ways and lead me into thy path.* The flesh is like the body. No amount of preservatives will keep it. It must soon decay. When you seek to preserve the flesh, its rottenness will spring forth. You'll be surprised how obnoxious it can get. Kill it, don't preserve it. Kill and bury it and let God be risen in its stead. Jesus wants to be fully formed in you.

You may be saying, "How am I to know what needs to be crucified? How am I going to kill it? I need help to do it." Consider the words, *"all flesh is as grass"* (1 Peter 1:24a, KJV). Harvested wheat must go through a process that separates it from the tiers (chaff), which aren't good for eating. God takes us through a process of threshing and winnowing to separate the wheat from the tiers in our lives. I see in His hand a winnowing fork. He is fanning with challenges, big and small, verbal and nonverbal, intrapersonal and interpersonal, to allow you to see the tiers and surrender them to His unquenchable fire to be consumed. The wind of the winnowing fork is making the tiers quite visible. Satan, on the other hand, doesn't want you to recognize the tiers, or little things, in your life that aren't pleasing to God. But God wants you to see them so that you can submit them to the refiner's fire.

Listen to the words of the psalmist:

> "Give me understanding, so that I may keep your law and obey it with all my heart. Direct me in the path of your commands, for there I find delight. Turn my heart toward your statutes and not toward selfish gain … Though the arrogant have smeared me with lies, I keep your precepts with all my heart. Their hearts are callous and unfeeling, but I delight in your law. It was good for me to be afflicted so that I might learn your decrees. (Psalm 119:34–36, 69–71)

Any branch that doesn't produce good fruit must be pruned. If only the stump remains, rejoice, because it will soon spring forth more beautiful fruit than before. Be fruitful in the years to come. Let God arise in you, and the enemy of your soul scatter. Here's a short prayer of surrender that you can now say:

Lord, I surrender my weakness, my fears, my sorrows, and my pains for the joy of the Lord. I say yes to you and to your ways, Lord, in Jesus's name.

Let's shake the wheat off and gather the tiers for the fire. Allow God to burn away the dross inside. His refiner's fire will do it for you. Your suffering is not unto eternal damnation, but unto redemption. His winnowing fork and refiner's fire will do it for you. He wants to make you holy in the process of your suffering that you finish well.

If you don't know that you have a problem, you'll never know that Jesus can solve it. God is able to solve all your problems, no matter how difficult you think they might be. Put Him to the test. Hand them over to Him. God is not vexed with us because we messed up. He loved us even before we got saved. The price for sin has already been paid through the blood of Jesus Christ. If you've already asked Jesus Christ to come into your life and have accepted Him as your Lord and Savior, the challenge now is for you to kill the "flesh" and walk as a redeemed child of the kingdom of God. In that walk of faith in Jesus Christ, we experience suffering that frees us from sin. If you've never given your life to the Lord, simply say this prayer: *Lord Jesus, I surrender to you now. Forgive me of all my sins and cleanse me from all unrighteousness. Thank you for receiving me, and make me your child, in Jesus's name. Help me to live my life pleasing to you. Amen.*

Chapter Eight: Suffering Frees Us from Sin

The price for spiritual success is costly, and many consider it too dear to be paid. Yet many of us are all too willing to pay a huge price for great fame, fortune, and other fleshly desires: the lusts of the flesh, the lusts of the eyes, and the pride of life. We surrender eternal life for temporal success:

> "Therefore, since Christ suffered in his body, arm yourselves also with the same attitude, because whoever suffers in the body is done with sin. As a result, they do not live the rest of their earthly lives, for evil human desires, but rather for the will of God." (1 Peter 4:1–2)

Suffering provides a way of pruning (John 15:1–2). The most fruitful lives are those that our heavenly Father has pruned through the process of tribulation, suffering, or even death. The hotter the battle, the sweeter the victory. God allows tragedy in our lives to cause us to look to heaven for salvation and not to ourselves. God is ridding us of bad habits, thoughts, and dependencies, making us more fruitful (Colossians 3:1, 5, 8–10). He encourages us to *"Endure hardship as discipline"* (Hebrews 12:7a).

We need to die to ourselves and our own desires before God can use us.

> *"… unless a kernel of wheat falls to the ground and dies, it remains only a single seed. But if it dies, it produces many seeds"* (John 12:24).

Sometimes we must step aside in order for God's greater works to be done. Jesus had to go away for God's greater good to be manifested: "*... it is for your good that I am going away. Unless I go away the Advocate will not come to you; but if I go, I will send him to you*" (John 16:7). Persecution is part of God's plan to help us mature in all aspects of life. Jesus said:

> "*Blessed are those who are persecuted because of righteous-ness*" (Matthew... 5:10).

Adversity often happens to the godly as a means of providing greater visibility of God's kingdom and righteousness. Before His death, Jesus said to the disciples:

> "All this I have told you so that you will not fall away. They will put you out of the synagogue; in fact, the time is coming when anyone who kills you will think they are offering a service to God. They will do such things because they have not known the Father or me. I have told you this, so that when their time comes you will remember that I warned you about them ..." (St. John 16:1–4)

In this case, the disciples were pre-warned so that they would understand what was happening and wouldn't sin by turning away from God. God also allows hardship to show us how to turn our grief to joy.

> "Very truly I tell you, you will weep and mourn while the world rejoices. You will grieve, but your grief will turn to joy. A woman giving birth to a child has pain because her time has come; but when her baby is born she forgets the anguish because of her joy that a child is born into the world. So with you: Now is your time of grief, but I will see you again and you will rejoice, and no one will take away your joy." (St. John 16:20–22)

God may also allow situations in our lives to worsen to teach us greater responsibility and obedience. With reference to Jesus, the writer of Hebrews noted that though He was God's Son on earth, He learned obedi-ence through His suffering (5:8). It was the practical outworking of a heart of obedience to God Almighty. This may also involve financial constraints (Luke 16:10–12).

The Lord uses great challenges to prepare us for leadership. Such was the circumstance when Jesus turned to the crowd and said:

> "If anyone comes to me and does not hate father and mother, wife and children, brothers and sisters—yes, even their own life—such a person cannot be my disciple. And whoever does not carry their cross and follow me cannot be my disciple. Suppose one of you wants to build a tower. Won't you first sit down and estimate the cost to see if you have enough money to complete it? For if you lay the foundation and are not able to finish it, everyone who sees it will ridicule you, saying, "This person began to build and wasn't able to finish." (Luke 14:26–30)

God often uses adversity to accomplish His greater purposes. We trust that this book is giving you more insight into how the Lord uses everyone and everything for His sovereign purposes.

God used the betrayal of His Son to bring great glory to His name. Paul referred to this as "... *God's wisdom, a mystery that has been hidden and that God destined for our glory before time began. None of the rulers of this age understood it, for if they had, they would not have crucified the Lord of glory*" (1 Corinthians 2:7–9). We need the wisdom and strength of God to endure betrayal.

The threshing and winnowing processes separate the things that cling to us that aren't good, while the pruning process trims us so that we become more like Jesus. It's the work of God to develop His strength in us and mold us with His character and in His appearance so that we can serve Him for eternity. In living as children of the kingdom of God, there is a place for us to learn to embrace suffering, which God allows to come upon us. It compels our eternal destiny. Let's look more closely at how this happens.

Chapter Nine: Suffering Compels Your Eternal Destiny and the Kingdom of God

"… Seek ye first the kingdom of God, and his righteousness; and all these things [that are not priority in the kingdom] shall be added unto you" (Matthew 6:33).

"For the Kingdom of God is not a matter of eating and drinking, but of righteousness, peace and joy in the Holy Spirit" (Romans 14:17).

In other words, kingdom priority is not your daily physical needs, or even your health, wealth, and prosperity. Its righteousness, peace, and joy in the Holy Ghost. They are the eternal things we should seek as Christians. We look not on the things of this world that are temporary, but rather on the eternal things (2 Corinthians 4:18). God allows suffering, and even death, to get us into the place where our eternal destiny is compelled by the things we suffer. He sacrifices the temporary for the eternal.

Jesus gave His physical life to gain sons and daughters in glory:

"For God so loved the world that he gave his one and only Son, that whoever believes in Him shall not perish but have eternal life" (John 3:16).

Jesus gave up His physical life so that we can obtain life in His kingdom.

Suffering transforms our prayer life into one of selflessness and godliness. It takes us into the heart of God, where it's no longer our will or desire, but God's. Jesus experienced this when He was in the garden suffering physical and emotional agony. He reached the point where He said,

"*Not my will, but thine, be done*" (Luke 22:42).

Had Jesus aborted the cross by having His own way, salvation would not have come to mankind. God's kingdom would not be available to us.

> Hannah experienced a similar transformation in prayer as she travailed over her barrenness before God. She came to the point where she agreed to give her son to God, should God bless her with one. She must have felt the heartbeat of God as she struggled and thought it appropriate to offer her son to the work of ministry for God's kingdom. Samuel became one of God's most powerful prophets. Many victories were secured for the kingdom because of his ministry. In fact, Hannah was greatly rewarded, because God opened her womb and gave her five more children thereafter (1 Samuel 2:20–21). Her suffering compelled her to seek God's kingdom first, and God blessed her with her desire because it was in line with His kingdom plan. Note that it was God who closed her womb in the first place: "And her adversary also provoked her sore, for to make her fret, because the Lord had shut up her womb" (1 Samuel 1:6, KJV).

Suffering at times precedes a change of season in our lives. Your rejection is a sign of new season in your life. In Genesis 41–47, we read the story of Joseph. He was rejected by his brothers, who eventually sold him into slavery in Egypt. He even ended up in jail. Through God's divine intervention, he interpreted Pharaoh's dream and was given a place of prominence in the service of Pharaoh, king of Egypt. Joseph was put in charge of the whole land of Egypt, and later he was able to save his father and brothers when there was a famine in the land.

KINGDOM PRIORITIES

Solomon prayed for wisdom to lead God's people. God's wisdom is an imperative to the righteousness, peace, and joy of His kingdom. As a consequence, not only was he the wisest man ever to live, but he was also the wealthiest (1 King 3:7–13). Solomon recognized more than most others that the things of life were vanity and had no eternal value. Only those things that pertain to the kingdom of God will last forever.

We ask amiss when our priority is not kingdom-based. Your priority must be God's priority, irrespective of your physical or temporal needs. Everything else must be secondary. Jesus taught His disciples this prayer:

> *"Our Father in heaven, hallowed be your name, your kingdom come, your will be done, on earth as it is in heaven. Give us today our daily bread"* (Matthew 6:9–11).

Our daily bread became secondary in contrast to the kingdom priority needs. God's kingdom is everlasting and demands our focus.

Jesus demonstrated this focus on eternal priorities in His time of physical need in the wilderness (Matthew 4:1–11). There, He was led by the Spirit to be tempted and could have succumbed to Satan, the prince of the world. However, He chose the eternal things of God instead of that which satisfies the flesh. Jesus learned obedience by the things He suffered (Hebrews 5:8). God's kingdom needs to be our priority. Paul said in Galatians 2:20: "*I have been crucified with Christ and I no longer live, but Christ lives in me.*" He also said, "*… though our outward man perish, yet the inward man is renewed day by day*" (2 Corinthians 4:16, KJV).

WISDOM: PAIN THAT IS HIDDEN IS HARDLY HEALED.

> "Therefore confess your sins [hurts, pains, weakness, and suffering] to each other and pray for each other so that you may be healed" (St. James 5:16a)

Bring your cares to the Lord Jesus Christ, or even those appointed by God. We fail to come to God because we're so broken and don't understand that our brokenness makes us better candidates for His love and power:

"And call on me in the day of trouble; I will deliver you, and you will honor me" (Psalm 50:15).

Chapter Ten: Rejection in Suffering

Your rejection is a sign of a new season in your life. Mary was put aside because she was anointed to bear the Christ child.

Joseph was rejected in order to become who God ordained him to be, a deliverer.

The lepers were outside the gate of Jerusalem so that God could use them to free Jerusalem from poverty.

The stone the builder rejected has become the chief cornerstone. Jesus was described in scripture as the stone the builder rejected.

> "To you then who believe, he is precious; but for those who do not believe,
>
> The stone that the builders rejected has become the very head of the corner." (I Peter 2:7 NRSV)

It should be encouraging know that Jesus himself encountered rejection. He was rejected when He came to His own people and they would not receive Him.

> "He was despised and rejected by mankind, a man of suffering, and familiar with pain. Like one from whom people hide their faces he was despised, and we held him in low esteem". (Isiaah 53:3 NIV.)

On the cross Jesus felt the pain of being cut off from His heavenly Father.

"…My God, my God why has thou forsaken me?" (Matt. 27:46 KJV).

The bible tells the reason for every suffering that Jesus went through, even his rejection by men and being forsaken by God, the Father.

> "Yet it was the Lord's will to crush him and cause him to suffer, and through the Lord makes his life an offspring for sin, he will see his offspring and prolong his days; the will of the Lord will prosper in his hand." (Is 53:10 NIV)

We were all created for God's glory. However, God knew that only Jesus can bring us back from our fallen position and make us once again His offspring.

> "…Fear not: for I am with thee: I will bring thy seed from the east, and gather thee from the west; I will say to the north, give up; and to the south, keep not back: bring my sons from far, and my daughters from the end of the earth; Even everyone that is called by my name: for I have created him for my glory, I have formed him; yea, I have made him." (Is. 43:7-10KJV.)

God's ultimate purpose is for all of his creation to manifest His Glory, and He chooses the path to accomplish this.

God has put me aside in the backside of the desert of unemployment to prepare me for my next dimension in Him. This is where I am learning to wait patiently and walk humbly before Him.

God will put you out of your own family in order to raise you up to be their deliverer.

Your disappointment is a set-up for God's appointment.

Every trial, tribulation, persecution, sickness, disease, or even death provides spiritual benefits. God works them for our good. What virtues can ensue from these challenges?

Chapter Eleven: Suffering for Sanctification

Most of us want God to use us, but few want to surrender. We must die to self for God to be able to trust us with His mighty powers. The sooner we die, the better it is for the kingdom of God, because the sooner we come into the fullness of Christ. Christ is being formed in us, and it's a process. We've all heard the saying, "Patience is a virtue." We must allow this virtue to have its perfect work in our lives (James 1:4).

Tribulations are designed to give us patience in order for us to accomplish the will of God. We have nothing to lose when we suffer for Christ. It's just the cost we pay for the prize. It cost Jesus everything. It cost us only our flesh. What we're asked to give up is nothing compared to what God is offering us—His glory.

Oswald Chambers in his book *My Utmost for His Highest* gave an exegesis of the passage, "We were therefore buried with him through baptism into death in order that, just as Christ was raised from the dead through the glory of the Father, we too may live a new life."[2] (Romans 6:4). Chambers goes on to say that no one experienced complete sanctification without going through "white funerals" —the burial of the old life. If there has never been the crucial moment of change through death to the self, sanctification will never be anything but an elusive dream. There must be a white funeral, a death with only one resurrection—a resurrection into the life of

---

2 When we are baptized in water, it signifies that we were buried with Christ. Our old ways of living were buried: we die to our selfish ways. We are now free to live in the resurrection power of Christ.

Jesus Christ. Nothing can defeat a life like this. It has oneness with God for only one purpose … to be a witness for Him.

Dying to the self will give rise to resurrection and newness, the Christ life, the same life that Christ lived. Unless we die to the flesh, we will never be able to live the life that Christ died for us to live.

Chapter Twelve: The Greater Glory Revealed

The Glory of His Suffering

The greater the degree of suffering that we are experiencing, the greater the glory to be revealed in our lives. That glory is the light that will shine in the darkness of our suffering. The light shines brightest in our darkness, and the darkest hour is just before dawn, the point at which we experience relief from suffering.

For the light of the glory of God to be revealed (shine bright) in our hearts, we must first crucify the flesh in our hearts (2 Corinthians 4:6–15).

> "For our light affliction, which is but for a moment, worketh for us a far more exceeding and eternal weight of glory; While we look not at the things which are seen, but at the things which are not seen: for the things which are seen are temporal; but the things which are not seen are eternal." (2 Corinthians 4:17–18, KJV)

The things we suffer for Christ in this life are not worthy to be compared with the glory that shall be revealed as a result (Romans 8:18).

Weeping may endure for a night, but joy comes in the morning. There is joy unspeakable and full of glory awaiting at the end of all suffering. The restoration of Christ's glory was only attainable after His death, burial, and resurrection (Romans 8:14–30).

The Spirit leads us through these difficult times and brings us into victory. The Spirit led Jesus into the wilderness to be tempted by the devil. God is working out His purpose in your life and mine to fulfill His glory in us.

The Holy Spirit will indeed lead us where our trust is without borders and allow us to walk upon waters when we call upon Him in truth. The Spirit will take us deeper than our feet could ever wander, and cause our faith to be made stronger through Jesus Christ. God's grace abounds in deepest water. *"But where sin abounded, grace did much more abound"* (Romans 5:20). He gives more honor to those who are weak among us.

Chapter Thirteen: You Are God's Masterpiece

"He has made everything beautiful in its time" (Ecclesiastes 3:11a).

One night, I had a vision of myself painting the inside of a wall with a paint mixture that had a wrong color blend. The paint container held the evidence that the blend was inconsistent; however, I continued painting. To my surprise, eventually the wall miraculously transformed into a most beautiful masterpiece of fine art. This was reproduced every time I painted a wall.

In spite of the outcome of the choices we make in our lives, God is able to make us into His great masterpiece. Our lives are like big paintings created by God. He knows how to blend the color of our lives with the correct lighting and consistency in order to produce treasures. What a marvelous truth! The Lord God said to the Israelites, *"Now if you obey me fully and keep my covenant, then out of all nations you will be my treasured possession"* (Exodus 19:5a). As children of God, Jews and Gentiles who through faith in Jesus Christ have been grafted in, we are God's greatest treasure. No diamond, ruby, or pearl is more precious than His children. We are God's jewels. God knows how to make our lives beautiful. He affords us the opportunity to die so that He, in all His beauty, can live in us. Now that is glorious!

Michelangelo, the great sculptor, was asked how he managed to create his finest masterpiece, "David." He responded by saying, "It was easy. 'David' was already in the stone. All I did was chip away that which was not him" (https://quoteinvestigator.com). God does the same with us. Because we're born again, our lives are etched in Christ, who is in us. As we die daily, the life of Christ in us will be more visible. His light will shine brighter in us, reflecting His glory. *"For we who are alive are always being given over to death for Jesus' sake, so that His life may be revealed in our mortal body"* (2 Corinthians 4:11).

Death is essential to life. Paul wrote in Galatians 2:20–21:

> "I have been crucified with Christ and I no longer live, but Christ lives in me. The life I live in the body, I live by faith in the Son of God, who loved me and gave Himself for me. I do not set aside the grace of God ..."

Faith in God and His grace form the basis of what God does for us, rather than what we do for ourselves. God loves us more than we can imagine. Our love for God is no match for His love, but He still requires it of us: *"This is love, not that we loved God, but that He loved us and sent His Son as an atoning sacrifice for our sins"* (1 John 4:10). God's love for us is perfect. He loves us in spite of ourselves.

We are God's most precious creation. Soon we will be flawless and will recover the glory humanity had before the fall of Adam. God made every living and moving thing according to their kind (Genesis 1:20–21). However, when He made us (mankind), we were made according to His image and likeness (Genesis 1:26–27). No other creature was ever created in this way. This is so awesome that, in fact, the psalmist David wrote: *"what is mankind that you are mindful of them, human beings that you care for them? You made them a little lower than the angels and crowned them with glory and honor"* (Psalm 8:4–5).

We are *"fearfully and wonderfully made"* (Psalm 139:14), but we must not judge ourselves by our outward appearance. Speaking of the lilies of the field, Jesus said: *"not even Solomon in all his splendor was dressed like one of these"* (Matthew 6:29b). Jesus was addressing outward apparel, but the true man lies within the body, so *"Though outwardly we are wasting away, yet inwardly we are being renewed day by day"* (2 Corinthians 4:16b). We have the DNA of God. God's divine nature is assigned to us and no other creatures on earth. As we turn to God, allowing Him to take His rightful place in us, He brings out His true nature from within. We are God's workmanship created in Christ Jesus unto good works (Ephesians 2:10). God is working out His purposes in our lives. We have this treasure in earthen vessels (2 Corinthians 4:7). God made us that way so that excellence of His power, when manifested, would be made known to be of Him and not of us.

Chapter Fourteen: Embracing Your Suffering

We can see the importance of embracing suffering based on the benefits highlighted in previous chapters. In embracing our suffering, we enter into a deeper understanding of the sufficiency of God's grace, which is more than enough for us.

Paul experienced this grace of suffering when he asked the Lord to take away a thorn in the flesh three times. The Lord responded by saying that His grace was sufficient for Paul. Paul learned that at his weakest, God's strength was increasingly made perfect. As a result, he was able to say that he could *"glory in tribulations"* (Romans 5:3, KJV). What a realization, or what I would call experiential knowledge!

Consider Shadrach, Meshach, and Abednego, who refused to bow to the king. They recognized the faithfulness of God and His ability to deliver; however, they also recognized the sovereignty of God and declared that even if God didn't deliver them, they wouldn't bow. This is overcoming faith. They loved not their lives even unto death. What tremendous faith! God didn't deliver them from the king. They were thrown into the fiery furnace, but what happened after was awesome. In the midst of their ordeal, they encountered a fourth man in the furnace. Jesus was present with them and was seen by the king. What a tremendous testimony! Their worst test became their greatest testimony.

The Lord promised to be with us at all times. He won't leave us when we need Him the most.

The psalmist David said:

> "O Lord, thou hast searched me, and known me. Thou knowest my downsitting and mine uprising, thou understandest my thought afar off. Thou compassest my path and my lying down, and art acquainted with all my ways. For there is not a word in my tongue, but, lo, O Lord, thou knowest it altogether. Thou hast beset me behind and before, and laid thine hand upon me. Such knowledge is too wonderful for me; it is high, I cannot attain unto it. Whither shall I go from thy spirit? or whither shall I flee from thy presence? If I ascend up into heaven, thou art there: if I make my bed in hell, behold, thou art there. If I take the wings of the morning, and dwell in the uttermost parts of the sea; Even there shall thy hand lead me, and thy right hand shall hold me. If I say, Surely the darkness shall cover me; even the night shall be light about me. Yea, the darkness hideth not from thee; but the night shineth as the day: the darkness and the light are both alike to thee. For thou hast possessed my reins: thou hast covered me in my mother's womb. I will praise thee; for I am fearfully and wonderfully made: marvelous are thy works; and that my soul knoweth right well." (Psalm 139:1–14, KJV)

David is assured of God's presence throughout his entire life. God promises never to leave or forsake us.

Peter further admonished us:

> But let none of you suffer as a murderer, or as a thief or as an evildoer or as a busybody in other men's matter. Yet if any man suffer as a Christian, let him not be ashamed; but let him glorify God on this behalf. (1 Peter 4:15–16).

In our suffering as Christians, we are judged not unto condemnation but unto redemption. We are chastened based on what will benefit us the most. Our suffering comes as part of our Christian virtue and to reveal God's glory in our lives. It draws us closer to God and makes us more effective in ministry. The paradoxical truth is that if we avoid suffering as Christians, we are avoiding our spiritual growth and development.

Suffering as a non–Christian has the potential to compel destinies; however, it's important to determine whether God orchestrated the plan for your suffering or if it's purely due to sinfulness. Paul clearly stated:

> "… God is not mocked: for whatsoever a man soweth, that shall he also reap. For he that soweth to his flesh shall of the flesh reap corruption; but he that soweth to the Spirit shall of the Spirit reap life everlasting." (Galatians 6:7–8, KJV)

There's a direct correlation between the life one chooses to live and the consequences of our suffering; however, God is faithful, and if we confess our sins before Him, He will forgive them and cleanse us from all unrighteousness. The physical consequence of the sinful act may be a part of us sometimes, or even for a lifetime.

First the natural.

One of the reasons we die is to leave an inheritance for our children and our children's children. There are some things we cannot do while we're alive; for example, we cannot pass onto our children their inheritance.

> And for this cause he is the mediator of the New Testament, that by means of death, for the redemption of the transgressions that were under the first testament, they which are called might receive the promise of eternal inheritance. For where a testament is, there must also of necessity be the death of the testator. For a testament is of force after men are dead: otherwise it is of no strength at all while the testator liveth. Whereupon neither the first testament was dedicated without blood. (Hebrews 9:15–18, KJV)

Here the Lord uses a natural principle to explain a spiritual phenomenal. We're often admonished in scripture to leave an inheritance for our relatives after we die.

Chapter Fifteen: Death, the Ultimate Sacrifice/Choice

Many of us would like to encounter God's resurrection power, but we refuse to die. Whatever parts of our lives we surrender are the parts that God will resurrect. Jesus's sacrificial life led to His ultimate sacrifice—death. He laid down His life for us, and three days later, He rose to a new life by the resurrection power of God (John 2:19–21; Matthew 27:63, 28:1–6). He made the ultimate sacrifice and obtained resurrection glory.

Death is not final. For the person who has accepted Jesus Christ as Lord and Savior, as it was with Jesus, so it is for us. Death is a phase that we must all go through to enter into glory in heaven. Only born-again believers who are alive at the time of the rapture will escape death. We therefore do not need to fear death. We can say, "*O death, where is thy sting? O grave, where thy victory?*" (1 Corinthians 15:55, KJV). The sting of death is broken!

The pain that we encounter due to the death of our loved ones has its own purpose.

Even Enoch and Elijah, who did not die, will return and make that ultimate sacrifice. Why will they come and die? As a testimony of God's love and power—love for us His children, and the power of His resurrection.

When Jesus died, He paved the way for all mankind to have access to God. The veil of the temple was torn from top to bottom, indicating that God had made provision for all persons to come to Him through the blood of His Son, Jesus Christ. As a result of this, you and I have direct access to God when we choose to accept Jesus Christ as our Lord and Savior and die to self. When we die as children of God, we access the passage to glory that Jesus bought with His blood.

We all must pass through the valley of the shadow of death spiritually and physically in order to get to glory with the Father. We need not fear death and its shadow, because God is with us at all times. Jesus didn't just make the way for us to go to glory—He is the Way. Therefore, He is there with you on the path from life through death and into the glory of heaven.

THE MESSAGE OF SALVATION

The Real Reason Jesus Had to Die

Jesus died in order to satisfy the legal requirement of sin. In Genesis 2:16–18, God gave explicit instructions to Adam in the Garden of Eden: the moment they ate from the tree of the knowledge of good and evil, they would surely die. Death already had been created by God; however, it was powerless until Adam sinned by disobeying God. As long as Adam didn't touch that tree, death could not come to him. Although death existed, it was powerless. Death has no power or life of its own over the believer. It cannot kill without "legal rights" or permission. These rights provide open doors to Satan's kingdom. Death only came alive because of the curse of sin. Myles Munroe[3] in his teaching on why Jesus had to die points out three ways in which one dies. Based on scriptures, we know these to be true.

1. The departure of the Holy Spirit from the spirit of man.
2. The departure of man from God's presence
3. The departure of man's spirit from the physical body.

Death was only given power by the disobedience of man (Romans 5:12).

Death by sin was passed upon all men. It didn't come through man, but because of the act of sinful man.

---

3   Dr. Myles Munroe- Why Jesus had to die? You Tube, https://m.youtube.com. Posted July5, 2018

In order for God to rid us of death, He had to first solve the sin problem. We encounter death because of God's requirement for sin. Since His Word is exalted above His very name, He must ensure that whatever He said in the Garden concerning the punishment of sin is fulfilled (Psalm 138:2).

God will not speak a word that He will not fulfill, *so death is the natural result of the fulfilment of God's promise.* God gave rights to death to be alive after Adam sinned. The only way to avoid spiritual death is to avoid sin. But God has a plan to serve a blow to death and make it powerless again. Death is the evidence of sin in a person's life. In other words, death is the consequence of sin. God's mercy in sending Jesus didn't ignore death or the justifiable requirement of the law. Jesus, the only begotten Son of the Father, took our place, because death must be fulfilled in order to satisfy God's requirement of the law. Jesus paid the price for our sins. It cost Him dearly.

God said to Satan: "*And I will put enmity between thee and the woman, between thy seed and her seed; it shall bruise thy head and, and thou shalt bruise his heel*" (Genesis 3:15, KJV).

Jesus paid the penalty for sin in His human form, depriving Satan of power. The penalty for sin has been fully paid. Jesus's death destroyed Satan's power.

> Now if we be dead with Christ, we believe that we shall also live with him: Knowing that Christ being raised from the dead dieth no more; death hath no more dominion over him. For in that he died, he died unto sin once: but in that he liveth, he liveth unto God. Likewise reckon ye also yourselves to be dead indeed unto sin, but alive unto God through Jesus Christ our Lord. Let not sin therefore reign in your mortal body, that ye should obey it in the lusts thereof. (Romans 6:8–12)

Death has no mastery (power) over him.

> "Thou hast put all things in subjection under his feet. For in that he put all in subjection under him, he left nothing that is not put under him. But now we see not yet all things put under him. But we see Jesus, who was made a little

lower than the angels for the suffering of death, crowned with glory and honour; that he by the grace of God should taste death for every man." (Hebrews 2:8–9, KJV)

Jesus tasted death for all mankind. No one has to go to hell.

"The sting of death is sin; and the strength of sin is the law" (1 Corinthians 15:56, KJV).

God's solution to death is a promise of a seed that will crush the head of death. Jesus died for a greater purpose. The following are some of the reasons.

1. His substitution—Jesus was the substitution Lamb of God to take away our sins.
2. His flesh as man—Jesus had to come in the flesh to redeem mankind, as mankind had lost dominion to Satan because of Adam's disobedience to God.
3. Shedding of His blood—Jesus had to shed His blood, without which there would be no remission of sins.
4. He paid for sin—His sacrificial death paid the price for our sins; the wages of sin is death.
5. First fruit of our resurrection—Jesus was the first to be resurrected and ascend to God, the Father. We will soon follow in His footsteps.
6. To justify us—He satisfied the requirement of sin. We are justified because Jesus took our place and paid the penalty of sin for us.
7. To ultimately destroy the power of death—the death, burial, and resurrection of Jesus broke the power of sin over our lives. The sting of death, which is sin, is broken. Death has lost its power over us.

Jesus in death was separated from His Father as He took on the sins of the whole world.

"… My God, my God, why hast thou forsaken me?" (Matthew 27:46, KJV). He encountered spiritual death.

Jesus gave up the ghost and became separated from God as well as His physical body.

Chapter Sixteen: Divine Healing Belongs to God's Children

"*But he answered and said, It is not meet to take the children's bread and to cast it to dogs*" (Matthew 15:26, KJV). Jesus was saying that it's not right to take the children's bread and give it to strangers. It's God's will that we be healed of all our diseases.

Derek Prince[4], in one of his videos, spoke about barriers to our healing, which may also be extended to deliverance from evil and experiencing God's blessings. He highlighted the following as obstacles:

Ignorance—Isaiah 5:13; Hosea 4:6
Unbelief—Hebrews 13:12–13
Unconfessed sins—Proverbs 28:13; 1 John 1:9
Attitude of unforgiveness—Mark 11:25
Occult involvement—Exodus 23:24
Secret covenants—Free Masonry
Effects of curses—Generational

Jesus became our curse so that we can go free. He has given us power to pray for the sick.

> Now when the sun was setting, all they that had any sickness with divers diseases brought them unto him; and he

---

4   Derrick Prince – Invisible Barriers to Healing #4258, https://www.derekprince.org

laid his hands on every one of them, and healed them. And devils also came out of many, crying out, and saying, Thou art Christ the Son of God. And he rebuking them suffered them not to speak: for they knew that he was Christ. (Luke 4:40–41, KJV)

And Jesus answering saith unto them, Have faith in God. For verily I say unto you, That whosoever shall say unto this mountain, Be thou removed, and be thou cast into the sea; and shall not doubt in his heart, but shall believe that those things which he saith shall come to pass; he shall have whatsoever he saith. Therefore I say unto you, What things soever ye desire, when ye pray, believe that ye receive them, and ye shall have them. And when ye stand praying, forgive, if ye have ought against any: that your Father also which is in heaven may forgive you your trespasses. But if ye do not forgive, neither will your Father which is in heaven forgive your trespasses. (Mark 11:22–25, KJV)

DECLARATION

"Deal bountifully with thy servant, that I may live, and keep thy word" (Psalm 119:17, KJV).

And these signs shall follow them that believe; In my name shall they cast out devils; they shall speak with new tongues; they shall take up serpents; and if they drink any deadly thing, it shall not hurt them; they shall lay hands on the sick, and they shall recover. (Mark 16:17–18, KJV)

Sometimes the healing will be instantaneous; other times, we'll have to wait patiently upon the Lord. We must keep thanking God until we experience our healing.

Ask God to reveal any areas in your life where you are intentionally disobeying Him. As God reveals to you, allow your faith to arise and move into obedience. God will soon bring your healing and deliverance to you. You must worship God in the midst of your situations in order to receive your breakthrough, even as you wait upon Him. Many of us lose heart when we haven't seen immediate answers to our prayers. We must continue to plug into God by faith, believing what God is saying about our condition. The truth you know will set you free. The Holy Spirit reveals those things that God would like us to know.

> Howbeit when he, the Spirit of truth, is come, he will guide you into all truth: for he shall not speak of himself; but whatsoever he shall hear, that shall he speak: and he will shew you things to come. He shall glorify me: for he shall receive of mine, and shall shew it unto you. All things that the Father hath are mine: therefore said I, that he shall take of mine, and shall shew it unto you. (John 16:13–15, KJV)

We must maintain a good relationship with the Holy Spirit, for it is He who will reveal to us what God wants us to know concerning our situations. This way, we know what to pray for when we pray for our trials and tribulations.

BREAKING UNGODLY BELIEF

Every lie told to you by the devil must be exposed, renounced, and replaced by what God has said in order to break ungodly belief. We formulate ungodly belief by the lies we receive.

"The secret things belong unto the Lord our God: but those things which are revealed belong unto us and to our children forever, that we may do all the words of this law" (Deuteronomy 29:29, KJV).

There are things only God knows that concern Him greatly, and there are things that God Himself desires that we should know. When we believe the lies of the devil, our belief system becomes ungodly and interferes with our spiritual development as Christians. We're not able to attain the promises of God, because our flesh and spirit are filthy or contaminated.

"Having therefore these promises, dearly beloved, let us cleanse ourselves from all filthiness of the flesh and spirit, perfecting holiness in the fear of God" (2 Corinthians 7:1, KJV).

One way of cleansing ourselves from the filthiness of the flesh and spirit is to change what we believe about ourselves, God, and others. We are to take only what God says about Himself and us as the truth that will ultimately set us free. The Holy Spirit is commissioned to bring this truth to us through spiritual discernment and revelatory knowledge through dreams, visions, and reading God's Word.

Our experiences may seem to be true in our lives, but the greater truth centers around God's view of that situation or experience.

Unbelief blocks the flow of the Holy Spirit and prevents us from entering into the innermost being of God. God is inviting us into His presence, but we can be hindered by what we believe about Him, ourselves, and others.

Chapter Seventeen: We Have to Leave This World—Willing to Die

The willingness to lay down our lives will be made easier when we understand that the world we live in is at enmity with God. All the forces of evil are wrapped up in this world, so the love of this world equals enmity with God. We must love the world so that we may bring about eternal transformation, not in a manner that it changes us.

God's ultimate purpose is to take those He saved to His kingdom.

"... Lust of the flesh, and the lust of the eyes, and the pride of life, is not of the Father, but is of the world. And the world passeth away..." (1 John 2:16–17, KJV).

The love of the world is at enmity with God. We are not of this world. We have our home in heaven, where we must ultimately desire to be.

"They are not of the world, even as I am not of it." (John 17:16). We hate to leave this world because we love it and have fallen for its deadly charm. This world belongs to the devil, which is why it remains at enmity with God. The world, the flesh, and the devil are foes of heaven. Friendship with the world violates our marriage vows with heaven. Pleases read the following passages for further clarification; James 4:4, 3:3, 4:1–3.

Why would you love the world to the extent that you're unwilling to die? God's love for the world amounts to changing the world, not preserving its status quo. His love is designed to bring eternal transformation to those He snatches from it.

The devil is directing this world's course (Ephesians 2:1–3).

Reference to Satan, "In whom the god of this world hath blinded the minds of them which believe not, lest the light of the glorious gospel of Christ, which is the image of God, should shine unto them," (2 Corinthians 4:4 KJV)

We must fix our affection on heaven and the things of heaven, not on the earth. Heaven is Christ's place, the place where He dwells and where He wants us to be. The world is Satan's place. His power is here. To fix our hearts on the world is to be loyal to Satan. To fix our hearts on heaven is to be loyal to Christ. God's kingdom is not of this world. The Apostle Paul sums it up by saying that to be absent from this world is to be present with God (2 Corinthians 5:8).

We must choose to be present with God rather than remain in this world, because all this world has to offer is brokenness and strife.

Chapter Eighteen: Death, the Ultimate Healing

If given the choice of coming back to earth, those who died in the Lord would rather remain with Him. Because of the resurrection power of Christ, not only is Jesus our healer, but our resurrection and life. Jesus, speaking to Martha, said: "...I am the resurrection and the life: he that believeth in me, though he were dead, yet shall he live." (St. John 11:25 KJV)

Martha only understood Him to mean that in the last day, all of us would be raised to life from death. However, Jesus was referring to the truth that He has the power now to raise the dead. Many with doubt in their hearts have failed to believe God to restore their loved ones back to life. Also, many who have died, especially those who have battled sicknesses and disease for long periods of time, may not want to return to life, having experienced the bliss of heaven.

The ultimate healing is death. After death, you can no longer be sick or subjected to suffering. In the same way suffering frees us from sin, death frees us from sickness and disease.

God may choose to keep us from returning to life on earth, because He wouldn't want us to experience more than we can bear.

"*Precious in the sight of the Lord is the death of his saints*" (Psalm 116:15, KJV).

Many people might not want to continue living: "Women received their dead raised to life again: and others were tortured, <u>not accepting</u>

<u>deliverance</u>; that they might obtain a better resurrection" (Hebrews 11:35, KJV, emphasis added).

To not accept deliverance literally means not accepting redemption or the chance to be freed from the enemy of God who is inflicting punishment. In other words, the deliverance offered must be purchased at the price of constancy. Many born-again Christians, because of the height of the temptation and trials they endured, would refuse to return to earth if given the choice, in order not to fall prey to the forces of darkness. This is also faith in action, because they're looking for a better resurrection. There's much to gain in heaven, a far more appealing prospect when earthly gains are considered. They would rather die than surrender to earthy pressure to change their position in Christ.

According to Hebrews 11:35, it takes faith to believe God to raise your dead. But it also takes faith to refuse to compromise your Christian values and show that you "love not your life, even unto death."

We overcome even by doing what has been stated above.

"And they overcame him by the blood of the Lamb, and by the word of their testimony; and they loved not their lives unto the death" (Revelation 12:11, KJV).

Chapter Nineteen: Death, the Final Enemy Defeated

Jesus destroyed the power of death with His death; because of this truth, when you die, you will rise. Death has simply become a passageway.

The Bible says, "The spiritual did not come first, but the natural, and after that the spiritual."(I Corinthians 15:46). For every spiritual connotation, there's a natural scenario. In the same way that spiritual death will be ultimately destroyed and thrown in the Lake of Fire, so will natural death be given a death blow and be overcome by the resurrection.

To be absent from this life is to be present with God.

The spoils of death. Death has its own benefit. Jesus divided the spoils among us. We now have authority over the three keys of death, hell, and the grave, because Jesus went through all three for us at Calvary. Jesus had to die in order to bear the sins of many (1 Corinthians 15:20–26). He became the first fruit of many of us who will come after.

The last enemy to be defeated is death. God wants us to defeat all our enemies and finish our course with joy. All our enemies are supposed to be destroyed—poverty, generational curses, bitterness, evil speaking, and others.

After we die, we will rise. We will see our loved ones who have died in the Lord. No power on earth can hold us down.

Chapter Twenty: Heaven Belongs to You

"If we live, we live for the Lord, and if we die, we die for the Lord. So, whether we live or die, we belong to the Lord." Romans 14:8

When we belong to God, we will be where He is. Jesus promised that where he is there we will be also.

"But our citizenship is in heaven, and we eagerly await a savior from there, the Lord Jesus Christ, who, by the power that enables him to bring everything under his control, will transform our lowly bodies so that they will be like his glorious body." (Philippians 3:20-21). Your citizenship is in heaven if you belong to Jesus Christ.

You are not second-class citizens of heaven, but rather first-class. You are citizens of heaven and a royal priesthood. You are destined to judge angels (1 Corinthians 6:3–4).

You are seated with Christ in heaven. It's your rightful place of authority, the highest place in glory. Only God the Father sits higher than you. You are a co-laborer with Jesus Christ and joint heir to the throne of God.

"Ask me, and I will make the nations your inheritance, the ends of the earth your possession."(Psalm 2:8).

We have the right to come boldly to the throne of grace when we're going through suffering, because by God's grace we have been given free access through the blood of His son. We have been given unfettered access already. It has already been done. We are viceroys from heaven. We are rulers exercising authority on earth on behalf of heaven.

By asking, seeking, and knocking, we prepare ourselves for the things God has for us. It's simply a part of the process to prepare us. Heaven is God's throne, and the earth is His footstool. We are seated with Him in heavenly places, so the earth is our footstool as well. We must operate from our heavenly place of authority in Christ Jesus. Our suffering compels this destiny.

The reason for the process of suffering is so we don't ask amiss and misuse or abuse God's precious commodities. The greatest of those is the blood of His Son, Jesus Christ. If we have the blood, we have everything. The blood of Jesus is the most potent and cherished commodity in heaven, and it's at our disposal. We alone can truly apply the blood of Jesus Christ. We do so by "sprinkling"[5] as we declare its power. (Hebrews 9:11–21).

We fight the good fight of faith as we go through our suffering. We can only succeed as we fight with heavenly armor and weapons (2 Corinthians 10:1–6).

When we learn to fight, we experience the sweetness of the process of our suffering, even our judgment (Revelation 10:9–10; Psalm 19:10; Proverbs 24:13; Jeremiah 15:16).

In Ezekiel, the scroll in his mouth tasted as honey, although bitter. "*And he said unto me, Son of man, cause thy belly to eat, and fill thy bowels with this roll that I give thee. Then did I eat it; and it was in my mouth as honey for sweetness*" (Ezekiel 3:3). The Word of God, which is the sword of the Spirit, is sweet in our mouth.

For John, writing in Revelation 10:9–10, the first sweetness was changed to bitterness as soon as he had eaten it. After the first ecstatic joy passed, the former sense of the awfulness of the work returned.

---

5   In the Old Testament of the bible we saw where Moses and other High Priests sprinkled the blood of animals on the people and anything that is to be cleansed. It's based on a covenant that God made with the Children of Israel. This ceremonial act depicts cleansing from sin and evil contamination. We sprinkle the blood of Jesus Christ by declaring its power over anything that defiles or causes contamination.

In our suffering, God may even use demons to get us where He wants us to be. Dr. Jerry Johnson puts forward the following reasons in his book, *Christians and Demons*[6]:

1. For physical punishment in hope of restoration. When we continue to engage in activities that we know we ought not to be doing, God at some point may choose to turn us over to Satan for our own good.

2. To remind other believers of the severity of discipline enacted by God and the church when a true Christian sins, such as the fornicator in Corinth and false teachers in Ephesians (1 Timothy 1:18–20).

3. To reveal the character of true faith during trials, as in the cases of Job and Jesus (Matthew 4:1–11).

4. To humble arrogant Christians and remind them of their spiritual dependency, as happened to Peter (Luke 22:31–33).

5. To take unique, effective Christians to a new level of maturity and usefulness. This happened to Paul in God's laboratory of character building.

6. To reveal and mercilessly judge false Christians, such as Judas, and false teachings.

7. To remind us that God is sovereign and all powerful, and that He is the author and finisher of our faith (Hebrews 12:2).

Are we making any compromises that will give Satan access to our minds?

6   Dr. Jerry Johnson, Christians and Demons, Armed and Anchored for Spiritual Warfare: Crossroads Christian Communication Inc., January 1, 2013.

Chapter Twenty-One:
Hearing the Voice of
God in Our Suffering

"Enter into his gates with thanksgiving, and into his courts with praise" (Psalm 100:4a, KJV).

Praise and worship set the tone for His presence. If you were told that the leader of your nation was coming to visit you, you would rejoice. You would begin to speak well of them, especially if they were your favorite leader. As the leader entered your home, there would be some kind of excitement. As it is in the physical, even so is it in the spirit.

What happens when the leader is ready to speak? You remain quiet and listen, because you want to get the most of what is being said. So is it with God, but even more so. He said, *"Be still, and know that I am God"* (Psalm 46:10a, KJV). Only God is to be worshiped and adored. In fact, He dwells in the praises of His people. It's most important to praise Him and make a big deal out of His presence. But you must be quiet and be still. He has something to say that will revolutionize your life and equip you for taking the nations.

Be quick to hear and slow to speak in His presence. His voice makes the difference. He will only give you the tongue of the learned after you have learned. Be quiet before your God, and wait patiently for Him. He will strengthen your heart in the process. Take notes, meditate on what He is saying, and repeat it until you believe it.

When my call, cry, voice, and speech line up with my belief, then my faith is being activated. The woman with the issue of blood said in her heart (belief): "*If I may but touch his garment, I shall be whole*" (Matthew 9:21, KJV). Her belief was based on truth; however, she activated it by pressing through the crowd. She was desperate and purposeful.

Your faith is the tangible reality of what you hope will occur, or the fulfilment of God's promise. God cannot resist faith; it attracts His attention. Faith does not wait upon God. It is based on what God has already said. As long as you can now believe it and act upon it, it will work for you.

That is why we read in the Bible: "*Now faith is the substance of things hoped for, the evidence of things not seen*" (Hebrews 11:1, KJV). If you have faith, you have seen it in the spirit, not in the physical. And if you can see it in the spirit, you can claim it. The psalmist David said, "*I had fainted, unless I had believed to see the goodness of the Lord in the land of the living*" (Psalm 27:13, KJV). We must believe to see God's goodness in our situations. We must believe to see and get our heart's desires. God always responds to faith, although He may not always respond in the manner you are expecting, but He will certainly respond.

Daniel prayed to God for twenty-one days, thinking that God was late in answering him. However, the angel of the Lord came and explained what had happened that caused the apparent delay: "*Since the first day that you set your mind to gain understanding and to humble yourself before your God, your words were heard, and I have come in response to them*" (Daniel 10:12b).

The prophet Isaiah came to Hezekiah the king and told him that the Lord said he was about to die. He told him to put his house in order, because he was seriously ill and God had told Isaiah that he wouldn't recover. But Hezekiah knew God. He had a relationship with a God he knew was faithful and merciful. God is touched with the feelings of our infirmities. Hezekiah turned to the wall, where he had nothing left but humility before God, and prayed. The Lord answered his prayer and caused the prophet to give him another word. The Bible said, "*This is what the Lord, the God of your father David, says: I have heard your prayers and seen your tears; I will heal you*" (2 Kings 20:5).

Chapter Twenty-Two: Seek the Counsel of the Lord

"Hear counsel, and receive instruction, that thou mayest be wise in thy latter end. There are many devices in a man's heart; nevertheless the counsel of the Lord, that shall stand" (Proverbs 19:20–21, KJV). We must seek to reconcile our desires with God's desires.

Psalm 37:1–24 highlights trust, delight, desires, commitment, and patience. Things to avoid include worry, anger, wrath, and evil. Our hope must be in God at all times.

Jesus understands things according to an eternal perspective. Having a godly perspective in your suffering is priceless. Jesus in His suffering asked that not His will but God's be done. We must seek godly counsel from those who have already received God's grace in their suffering. Their experience will teach us great wisdom and bring enormous peace in the midst of our storms.

Proverbs 1:1–33 is instrumental in our understanding of the significance of spiritual counseling. The passage points to the unwise one who refused godly counsel and was slain. The righteous who harken unto godly counsel shall dwell in safety and be free from the fear of evil. The fear of the Lord is the beginning of wisdom. Let us fear God only and live, experiencing the glorious liberty of life in Christ Jesus.

Chapter Twenty-Three:
The Glory of a Dying Soul

It is a glorious experience to witness a saint pass from this life into eternity. Some of our loved ones who have passed away were never healed of their illnesses, but the glory they experienced in passing was awesome to encounter for those by their bedside at the time of their transition. You can get a glimpse of that glory in the face of death. For those dying in Christ, it is glorious to behold such amazing expression on their faces and their in-depth act of worship.

To be absent from the body is to be present with God, which is why many would not venture to return, even if you were to pray the prayer for their resurrection. It's hard to taste the heavenly bliss and be willing to return to earth in your natural body, unless God intends it to be so.

Countless stories have been told of people who have had after-death experiences and obtained a glimpse of heavenly bliss. Others have seen visions of heaven that heightened their desire to be home with the Lord. However, God is always after His greatest glory. His ultimate desire is to reveal His glory for the whole world to see. His glory is revealed in us day by day. We are changed from glory to glory by His spirit. *"But we all, with open face beholding as in a glass the glory of the Lord, are changed into the same image from glory to glory, even as by the Spirit of the Lord"* (2 Corinthians 3:18, KJV).

"So we make it our goal to please him whether we are at home in this body or away from it" (2 Corinthian 5:9–10). The important question is: What

pleases God more? Is it being away from the body, or being in the body?

"Because of the Lord's great love, we are not consumed, for his compassion never fails." (Lamentations 3:22). God's mercy sustains us that we are not consumed. However, sometimes, because of the things we do in our bodies, we defile ourselves. As a result, it may be better for us to be absent from our bodies than to be in our bodies.

Death has no power. It has lost its sting. The sting is broken. The single most important question is: Will it be more pleasing to God for you to be in the natural or in the spiritual life? In other words, life after death. In what realm would you give Him greater delight and greater glory? Is God's purpose being fulfilled in your life?

Chapter Twenty-Four:
God's Grace Will Help You
Be Gracious to Others

The Care of Loved ones

SUFFERING PRODUCES GRACE THAT COMFORTS ALL

The pains that bind my family and friends together produce love and comfort emanating from God's grace in our lives.

"Comfort and pain are as old as the human experience, yet we struggle to understand their place in our lives and faith. Why do I not feel God's comfort? If He loves me, how could He let this happen?"[7]

For several months, I experienced excruciating pains in my joints and muscles. These pains originated from excessive usage of muscles that caused strains and arthritic conditions in my body. They were further aggravated by the degeneration of the bone structure that resulted in the most unusual feelings in my arms, neck, back and shoulders.

My wife and daughter became my nurses and prayer warriors. They developed the art of the masseuse. My mother, on the other hand, never ceased to pray. The whole family was indulged in my affliction in one way or the other. It brought us closer and created a tighter bond, love, and respect for each other. It taught us all true humility and grace. We are now more gracious than we have ever been because of my illness. Satan has lost this

---

7   Finding Comfort In Pain, LifeChurch.tv, August 26, 2016

battle and God has restored my body.

Dietrich Bonhoeffer, a German theologian sent a poem to his wife just months before he was hung in a Nazi prison.

"'Should it be ours to drain the cup of grieving,
Even to the dregs of pain,
At thy command,
We will not falter,
Thankfully receiving all that is given,
By thy loving hand.'"

These are comforting words from a man who understood the significance of his suffering.

The God we serve is the God of comfort in all our sufferings. Whatever you are going through right now provides a great opportunity for God to demonstrate this attribute of grace in your life. His strength is certainly being made perfect in our weaknesses.

> Blessed be God, even the Father of our Lord Jesus Christ, the Father of mercies, and the God of all comfort; Who comforteth us in all our tribulation, that we may be able to comfort them which are in any trouble, by the comfort wherewith we ourselves are comforted of God. For as the sufferings of Christ abound in us, so our consolation also aboundeth by Christ. And whether we be afflicted, it is for your consolation and salvation, which is effectual in the enduring of the same sufferings which we also suffer: or whether we be comforted, it is for your consolation and salvation. And our hope of you is steadfast, knowing, that as ye are partakers of the sufferings, so shall ye be also of the consolation. (2 Corinthians 1:3–7, KJV)

This passage depicts the Bible's greatest text on comfort. The word "comfort" occurs approximately ten times in one form or the other, whether in the noun form or the verb form. This represents about one-third of the thirty-one occurrences in the New Testament. The Apostle Paul spoke more about comfort and suffering than any other writer in the Bible. It's in this passage that he spoke the most about the subject. It's important to understand why Paul had to speak so much about suffering here. He was responding to his critics who thought that the sufferings that characterized his life were evidence that he wasn't an apostle.

This belief emerges in our present culture as well. There are many today, especially amongst evangelical churches, who believe that suffering characterizes those who are living in sin or unbelief. Nothing could be farther from the truth.

When God's grace of comfort is upon your life, it transcends everything you're experiencing in your suffering. You now only see Him, who is invisible, and cease focusing on your situation. This is where spiritual breakthroughs are birthed. When you allow God to be bigger than your situation, you will soon see His glory manifested in your life.

God's grace upon our lives is sufficient for us, and His sufficiency is more than enough. It's only by experiencing God's comfort in our sufferings that we're better able to comfort others in their own sufferings.

We suffer, therefore, not just for ourselves, but for others so that we can extend the comfort we receive from God to them.

Chapter Twenty-Five: The Accuser of the Brethren

Satan is the main accuser of the brethren. He provides opportunities for testing the believer. God's purpose for allowing these accusations is to settle the score with the devil by proving what's in our hearts. Although God can test us without using the accuser of the brethren, as He did with Abraham when He told him to sacrifice his son, he often uses the enemy to test us, like He did with Job. It is stated in Deuteronomy 8:1–3, 16 (KJV) that God tests us to see what's in our hearts:

> "All the commandments which I command thee this day shall ye observe to do, that ye may live, and multiply, and go in and possess the land which the Lord swore unto your fathers. And thou shalt remember all the way which the Lord thy God led thee these forty years in the wilderness, to humble thee, and to prove thee, to know what was in thine heart, whether thou wouldest keep his commandments, or no. And he humbled thee, and suffered thee to hunger, and fed thee with manna, which thou knewest not, neither did thy fathers know; that he might make thee know that man doth not live by bread only, but by every word that proceedeth out of the mouth of the Lord doth man live. ... Who fed thee in the wilderness with manna, which thy fathers knew not, that he might humble thee, and that he might prove thee, to do thee good at thy latter end."

The test demonstrates in an experiential manner whether or not we are applying biblical principles from the Word of God to our lives. In other words, it tells us whether we're living by faith or not. It also allows the Word of God to be tried in us to reveal our obedience or lack thereof.

The test is a legal requirement for all believers, and Satan knows this better than many of us, so he accuses us before God. He can only accuse us based on things we've done or said. There might be something God wants to prove in us, as in the case of Job. If this were not so, God would not have given in to Satan's accusations. If there were no legitimate reasons for Satan to accuse us, he couldn't do so unless God allowed it.

Our God is a righteous judge, and He judges everything according to His righteous judgment. Satan's accusation about Job is not unique to Job but is based on the fact that God wants to demonstrate our ongoing trust and confidence in Him. Like Job, we all tend to be self-righteous and lacking in humility, so God will allow our test to bring an affliction on us. This is not punitive because of sin but remedial to bring purification.

Many have argued that Job was tested because of his fear of God's judgment upon him. The Bible says that what he feared the most came upon him (Job 3:25). Fear is the opposite of faith in the life of the believer. The enemy will always capitalize when we're living in fear and not in faith. But did Job fear God in a negative way to have brought this on himself? Absolutely not. The Lord said in Job 2:3 that this destruction that came upon him was without a cause: "*In all this Job sinned not, nor charged God foolishly*" (Job 1:22, KJV).

At times God will test us to see what's in our hearts. He'll say to Satan, "Have you considered my servant (your name)?" God uses the enemy to bring storms and catastrophes into our lives to expose wickedness. Despite what has been stolen from us and all the enemy has done in our lives, God's great armies have preserved us. The caterpillar, the palmer worm, the canker worm all belong to God, to use as He sees fit. "*And I will restore to you the years that the locust hath eaten, the cankerworm, and the caterpillar, and the palmerworm, my great army which I sent among you*" (Joel 2:25, KJV).

He calls them His great army. God is ultimately in charge, and He does whatever pleases Him for His great honor and glory. He knows just what is best for us. God calls off His army after we've been tried and tested. To be prepared to be the true sanctuaries of God, we must be tested in the wilderness of our lives to see what's in our hearts. The test allows for absolute surrender to the Lordship of Jesus Christ and demonstrates that without God not only are we nothing, but we cannot do anything pleasing to Him.

To live lives that are pleasing to God, we must die to our own ways and surrender to His authority. This is why suffering is a spiritual requirement for every believer. Satan knows this. Sadly, not many believers know this truth. It's only after we suffer for a while that God establishes us in Him, as His Word would have been tried and tested in us. We need not worry whether or not the test is fair, because God sets the examination. He is the invigilator who makes sure that the settings are just right. He won't provide anything we cannot bear. We must be obedient to the call of God to suffer for the sake of Christ. Our willingness determines our attitude as we obey the call to suffer and wait upon the Lord. Our obedience determines our trust in a faithful God, as well as our passion to fulfill our destiny. Consider the apostles who were beaten for the sake of the gospel in Acts 5:41. They deemed it an honor and privilege to suffer for the name of Christ. This is what Jesus meant when He said to eat his flesh and drink his blood (John 6:56). Or, to put it more palatably, "Take up the cup of salvation."

The children of Israel murmured profusely during their wilderness experience, so God destroyed many of them because of their disbelief. In fact, except for Caleb and Joshua, none of the children of Israel who left Egypt entered the Promised Land. Only the children born in the wilderness entered the Promised Land.

As each individual appropriates to himself or herself the death, burial, and resurrection of our Lord Jesus Christ, the life of Christ becomes the very life and nourishment of their innermost being. Understanding and accepting this truth validates our passion to suffer for the sake of Christ, because His work on Calvary gives us newness of life in Him. As Christ suffered for us, we too must be prepared to share in His suffering to be partakers of His resurrection.

Satan, the accuser of the brethren, has been sacked:

> There is therefore, now no condemnation to them which
> are in Christ Jesus, who walk not after the flesh, but after
> the Spirit. For the law of the Spirit of life in Christ Jesus
> hath made me free from the law of sin and death. (Romans
> 8:1–2, KJV)

Satan no longer has a place in heaven, nor can he accuse us before God.
He has lost his place. Heaven needs no more contamination. The heavenly
things have already been cleansed and purified once and for all by the
blood of our Lord and Savior Jesus Christ, the Lamb of God that was slain.
Christ's blood has been applied to the mercy seat. We have access to God
through the blood of Christ. Jesus, the Lamb of God, has paid the price
for our sins and has settled any legal requirement. Thank God, the accuser
of the brethren has been cast down. Satan now tempts us as he tries to
win the battle of our minds, but he only succeeds when we're mindful of
earthly things.

> "For they that are after the flesh do mind the things of
> the flesh; but they that are after the Spirit the things of
> the Spirit. For to be carnally minded is death; but to be
> spiritually minded is life and peace. Because the carnal
> mind is enmity against God: for it is not subject to the law
> of God, neither indeed can be. So then they that are in the
> flesh cannot please God. But ye are not in the flesh, but
> in the Spirit, if so be that the Spirit of God dwell in you.
> Now if any man have not the Spirit of Christ, he is none
> of his. And if Christ be in you, the body is dead because
> of sin; but the Spirit is life because of righteousness. But if
> the Spirit of him that raised up Jesus from the dead dwell
> in you, he that raised up Christ from the dead shall also
> quicken your mortal bodies by his Spirit that dwelleth in
> you. Therefore, brethren, we are debtors, not to the flesh,
> to live after the flesh. For if ye live after the flesh, ye shall
> die: but if ye through the Spirit do mortify the deeds of

the body, ye shall live. For as many as are led by the Spirit
of God, they are the sons of God." (Romans 8:5–14, KJV)

Satan is defeated and has lost his place in heaven for good. He was only able to accuse us in heaven prior to the cross, because Jesus was not yet our advocate. The courthouse of heaven has no adversary, no accuser, but we can petition our cause before our loving Father with Jesus as our advocate, and the Holy Spirit as our counselor, comforter, and friend. We are judged so that we might be chastened by God our Father—not to be punished, but to be made perfect in holiness and sanctification by the Holy Spirit. The trial of our faith and our testings' only endear patience in us. This patience must have its perfect work in us, resulting in our perfection. Listen to what James, the apostle and brother of our Lord Jesus Christ, had to say: "*My brethren, count it all joy when ye fall into divers temptations; knowing this, that the trying of your faith worketh patience. But let patience have her perfect work, that ye may be perfect and entire, wanting nothing*" (James 1:2–4, KJV).

Chapter Twenty-Six: Being Equipped for His Glory

The Apostle Peter has this to say about the subject:

> "Beloved, think it not strange concerning the fiery trial which is to try you, as though some strange thing happened unto you: But rejoice, inasmuch as ye are partakers of Christ's sufferings; that, when his glory shall be revealed, ye may be glad also with exceeding joy. If ye be reproached for the name of Christ, happy are ye; for the spirit of glory and of God resteth upon you: on their part he is evil spoken of, but on your part he is glorified. But let none of you suffer as a murderer, or as a thief, or as an evildoer, or as a busybody in other men's matters. Yet if any man suffer as a Christian, let him not be ashamed; but let him glorify God on this behalf. For the time is come that judgment must begin at the house of God: and if it first begin at us, what shall the end be of them that obey not the gospel of God? And if the righteous scarcely be saved, where shall the ungodly and the sinner appear? Wherefore let them that suffer according to the will of God commit the keeping of their souls to him in well doing, as unto a faithful Creator." (1 Peter 4:12–19, KJV)

Learning to bear your own burden and the burdens of others equips you for carrying the weight of God's glory. Jesus learned obedience by the things He suffered. His ultimate learning experience was bearing the cross.

Why the need for us to bear our burdens when Jesus already carried them? Every flesh must have its own experience in the crucifixion to be a co-laborer or partaker of Christ's suffering. We must experience the sense of our own crucifixion with Christ. This is not as unto salvation, but by participation and equipping for more valuable service in the kingdom of God. For you to live, you must die. Galatians 2:20 rings true. You need experiential knowledge of your faith in Christ, which can only take place as you live out your life in trials and temptations. You must experience in your trials death to self—your ambition, desires, and own way of doing things. You must surrender all to the Lordship of Jesus Christ.

The trying of your faith works patience in your life. The greater the call of God upon your life, the greater will be the price to pay. The weight of God's glory depicts the heavy burden we must bear in our suffering and sacrificial life, if we are to be true bearers of His glory and presence. The "glory" in Hebrew is the *Doxa* of God. It is all that God is and possesses. It is of much weight, and we must learn how to bear it.

Learning to be obedient qualifies the call of God upon your life. God tries us before He increases His glory, or even His presence, in our lives. Abraham was asked to surrender His son as a sacrifice unto God. "*And he said, Lay not thine hand upon the lad, neither do thou anything unto him: for now I know that thou fearest God, seeing thou hast not withheld thy son, thine only son from me*" (Genesis 22:12, KJV).

We all must be tried and tested to see if we're living by faith. Job suffered the loss of his family and possessions. He was afflicted in his body, yet he said, concerning God, "*Thou he slay me, yet will I trust him*" (Job13:15, KJV). Will you still trust God in your infirmities or trials? We all must experience the partaking of Christ's suffering if we're to be true victors in Christ and reign with Him.

"*… as he is, so are we in this world*" (1 John 4:17, KJV).

Jesus had to suffer in this world, paying the price for our sins. He is our example in our suffering as we grow in faith to be like Him. Each of us must work out our salvation with fear and trembling as we embrace the process of surrendering our lives, laying our lives down to the obedience of Christ so that we might live glorious and victorious lives, often for the sake of others. In other words, sometimes we suffer as escape lambs for the punishment of others in order to bring them reconciliation.

It's part of being in a sinful world. We do not ignore the world around us. Jesus has done the greater part, so we need to follow in His footsteps and show love and mercy for the lost and dying world around us. Part of our suffering means enduring others around us in spite of their sinfulness. We must love them into the kingdom. We cannot see their needs unless we look beyond their faults. To love such people is sacrificial, in the same way God loves us and sent His only begotten Son to die for us. We too must love and demonstrate that quality in our lives.

Chapter Twenty-Seven: God Trains Our Hands to War

"Blessed be the Lord my strength, which teacheth my hands to war, and my fingers to fight: My goodness, and my fortress; my high tower, and my deliverer; my shield, and he in whom I trust; who subdueth my people under me". (Psalm 144:1-2, KJV)

"And from the days of John the Baptist until now the kingdom of heaven suffereth violence, and the violent take it by force" (Matthew 11:12, KJV). Taking territories for the kingdom is part of the spiritual life cycle of every believer. That makes us soldiers of war.

God wants us to contend for the things in our lives. He wants us to be in battle array, ready for battle. In our struggles, we learn how to fight and combat the forces of darkness in our lives. Our humility is wrought by our struggling to survive, with our dependency upon Almighty God. In our struggles, we learn how to wrestle the forces of darkness by applying biblical principles and strategies. We learn how to contend in battle. We learn how to fight the good fight of faith.

"See, it is I who created the blacksmith ..." (Isaiah 54:16).

Satan uses the very thing God created to harm us. He's a liar and a thief who only comes to steal, kill, and destroy our lives and families. We must rise up, take our rightful place in the Lord, and take back that which the enemy has stolen from us. Let us take hold of our inheritance. God will vindicate us in the process, but we must play our part and refute the lies of the enemy against us in order to obtain our final victory (2 Corinthians 10:3–6). Our journey is ordered by the Lord, and in order to enjoy it, we must first understand the process.

FROM GILGAL TO JORDAN

There's a process to get you into the place of final victory. Every believer has to be a part of this process. Like the children of Israel, we must be prepared to go through the various stages of the development of life. We must go from "Gilgal to Jordan." Two songs came to mind as I prepared to write this chapter.

First, Fanny Crosby's song, "In the Cross."

Jordan River is symbolic of that river that we must cross for our final victory and ultimate rest.

Secondly, Horatio Stafford's song, "It Is Well with My Soul." Whatever our portion be in life as a Christian we can most assuredly say, it is well.

Our Christian lives are lived out in cycles. We begin at Gilgal, as in Joshua 4 and 5 and 2 Kings 2:1-6. The Bible speaks to us as it is fulfilled in our Lord Jesus Christ. However, in order to get to Jordon, we must go through Bethel and Jericho as well.

WHAT HAPPENS AT GILGAL?

Jordan represents the place of testing of our faith. God will take us into the wilderness to see what's in our hearts. Crossing the Jordan of our lives is only a new beginning. Before we can actually claim and occupy the "Promised Land," we must battle the old giants of ourselves into submission. It reveals the true test of our faith. This is where Joshua and his army conducted their initial conquest of the Holy Land. We must learn to be victorious in our early battles, to set aside our old ways of living, our materialistic self. If we're to be promoted by God, we must be tried and tested in each stage. Gilgal is where it all started. It's the place of separation. It's a place of circumcision of the flesh or dying to our own selfish desires.

We must encounter our Gilgal to ensure that we are willing and capable of going on to Bethel, which will require greater sacrifice for the continued journey. We must prove ourselves in the test of time. What better way to do this than suffering for the sake of Christ? This is what will bring us into true surrender to Jesus Christ.

We must rise and take higher ground if we're to be successful in our Christian walk. We can't stay at Gilgal, for the Promised Land is not anywhere in sight. God has made us great and precious promises that we must apprehend and possess. It will require greater sacrifice than we can imagine. Some would dare to believe that we need not sacrifice, because Jesus has already done it all. However, the sacrifice required is brokenness before God in order to demonstrate true dependency on Him, the sovereign God.

WHAT HAPPENS AT BETHEL?

Bethel is the place of sacrifice. The sacrifice is not burnt offerings, but rather a sacrificial life. Bethel means "House of God," signifying the place where we encounter God the most in our lives. It's a place where sacrifices and vows are made to God to show our loyalty to and dependency upon Him. It's the place where deals are made with God.

When we go through suffering, we realize our need for God and are willing to make sacrifices to Him. This is an integral part of the process of our development as children of God. It's where God gets our attention the most. It's a place of ultimate surrender without any condition. We must be able to say like Job, "*Thou he slay me, yet will I trust in him*" (Job 13:15, KJV). This is where we learn that the things we cherished the most might not be what God ordered for us. God may not always give us what we want, but He will give us what is best for us. He chastens and disciplines us for the next phase of our journey as He takes us into warfare. Jericho represents the place of warfare in the Bible.

WHAT HAPPENS AT JERICHO?

After we've been brought by God to a place where we're fully committed to loving and serving Him, even unto death, He advances us on our journey. At Jericho, serious battles are fought and won for the sake of the kingdom of God. We would have learned from Bethel the significance of making sacrifice and being sold out to God: "*No man that warreth entangleth himself with the affairs of this life; that he may please him who hath chosen him to be a soldier*" (2 Timothy 2:4, KJV).

To be successful in the war, we must allow God to train our hands to fight. Our present warfare is not against flesh and blood, but rather against principalities and other evil spiritual beings (2 Corinthians 6:10).

At Jericho, the walls in our lives must come down. It's a place of intense battles to pull down strongholds and any remaining idols in our lives. It's a place where you rebuild life by laying proper foundations. What better time to fight the good fight of faith than when our backs are against the wall and only the "fittest of the fittest" will survive? The Africans have learned to fight spiritual warfare because it's a matter of life or death. They are up against serious demonic forces of darkness and Satanist activities. The hotter the battles are in our lives, the sweeter the victories. We must remember to put on the whole armor of God, as the weapons of this warfare are not carnal, but mighty through God to the pulling down of strongholds. See Ephesians 6:10-13. We must overcome Satan and his devices in order to transition to our next destination in our lives.

WHAT HAPPENS AT JORDON?

This takes us to our final destination in our cycle, the place of Jordan. Jordan means transition. Crossing the Jordan River for Joshua meant entering the Promised Land. This is where miraculous signs and wonders happen in the name of the Lord Jesus Christ. This is where immense supernatural breakthroughs will be wrought. This is where your struggles come to an end, only to start again when God desires to promote you to the next dimension in the Spirit. This is where Elijah transferred the prophetic mantle to

Elisha. This is where Moses handed over the leadership to Joshua. This is where Jesus was baptized.

The grace that saves will lead us to where God is taking us. Whatever we're going through right now, God's grace is still sufficient.

Finally, two things characterize what God does in our lives as He chastens us in our process. He does everything in His *time* and for His *glory*: *"For our light affliction, which is but for a moment, worketh for us a far more exceeding and eternal weight of glory"* (2 Corinthians 4:17, KJV).

Whatever God is doing in us will produce the changes He requires in His own time. Nothing happens to us except that which is allowed by God for the furtherance of His kingdom in our lives. God is kingdom oriented, and He works in us to bring His kingdom to bear in our lives:

"And we know that in all things God works for the good of those who love him, who have been called according to his purpose" (Romans 8:28). Whatever you're going through right now, God is working it out for your good. This could be some light afflictions that is just for a moment. "For our light and momentary troubles are achieving for us an eternal glory that far outweighs them all." (2Corinthians 4:17)

We must maintain the spheres of influence the Lord gives to us as we combat the forces of darkness in our lives. By His grace we maintain our authority within this sphere. Additionally, it is by His grace that this sphere will be greatly expanded so that we can take over more territories. With this in mind, we are better able to understand what Paul was saying in Philippians 4:13 (KJV): *"I can do all things through Christ which strengtheneth me."* "All things" refers to what needs to be done within your sphere, not outside of it. It is whatever God requires of you, not what you desire of your own free will. Many are disappointed because they lack understanding of this truth.

Chapter Twenty-Eight: The Names of Jehovah Revealed in Times of Need

The names of Jehovah have been revealed to God's children in the midst of their sufferings or times of need. **The names of God depict God's will for our lives and what He's willing to do for us when we desire His will to be done in our lives.**

The word "Jehovah" actually means, "To become," and it was a popular Hebrew name before God chose it. So when God chose this name for Himself, He was saying that He would "become" whatever was needed to fulfill His purposes in our lives. The translation "I AM" in Exodus 3 therefore implies, "I will become." We know that God is the great I AM, but we must also understand that He will become to us whatever is required to fulfill His purpose in our lives.

PROVIDER AT MOUNT MORIAH

In Genesis 22:13–14, Abraham is in crisis, needing a substitute sacrifice instead of his son. God provided a ram caught in the thicket. That was when God first became known as a provider—Jehovah Jireh. Do you have a dire need? He will show up just for you, if you accept Him as your provider. Abraham was faithful in believing God, and God was faithful in His faithfulness to him.

A HEALER IN THE HOUSE

In Exodus 15:26b (KJV), God makes a promise to the children of Israel in this revealing declaration about Himself: *"for I am the Lord that healeth thee."*

Do you know Him as your healer? You must first be in need to see the manifestation first-hand. He will be your healer if you believe and exercise your faith to receive from Him.

HE LEADS HIS CHILDREN IN BATTLE

In Exodus 17:8–15 (KJV), God intervenes in the life of the children of Israel and leads them into battle against their enemy, the Amalekites. God utterly annihilates Amalek and promises to *"put out the remembrance of Amalek from under the heaven"* (v. 14). What a great way to obtain a victory! Would you submit to Him today and allow Him to lead you through this fight? Moses built an altar in memory of this great victory and named it Jehovah Nissi, because the Lord had promised to fight his battle. God will lead you into your fight if you allow Him. He longs for you to know Him as the mighty banner.

HE IS PEACE TO THOSE IN NEED

In Judges 6:24, Gideon experiences tremendous fear after seeing an angel of the Lord face to face. The Lord immediately alleviates his fear by saying, *"Peace be unto thee; fear not: thou shalt not die"* (Judges 6:23, KJV).

Whatever situation you're facing right now, the peace of God is with you. Jesus lives in you. Gideon built an altar in memory of this event and called it Jehovah Shalom. No man can take away His peace. Ask God to manifest His peace in your heart and mind.

JESUS THE GOOD SHEPHERD

In Psalm 23:1, a well-known passage of scripture, David makes a solemn declaration based on God's revelation. He declares that God is his shepherd. The Message Bible reads:

> God, my shepherd! I don't need a thing. You have bedded
> me down in lush meadows, you find me quiet pools to
> drink from. True to your word, you let me catch my breath
> and send me in the right direction. (MSG)

God is the good shepherd. He is our Jehovah Roah, our shepherd. He will never lead us astray. You can trust Him today. He is the same yesterday, today, and forever.

OUR RIGHTEOUSNESS.

In Jeremiah 23:6, the prophet prophesied that the day was coming when God would save His people and they would dwell safely with Him. Jeremiah further stated that His name would be called, "The Lord Our Righteousness," which in Hebrew is Jehovah Tsidkenu. This righteousness has been instilled upon us who believe, and now we have become the righteousness of God in Jesus Christ. God has made you His righteousness. He has made you into what you are, because our righteousness is like filthy rags. Now when God sees us, He doesn't see us in our sinful state, but rather as sons and daughters, just like His begotten Son, Jesus Christ. What an awesome privilege to be God's righteousness on earth! Do you have a great relationship with your heavenly Father? He has saved you for His purpose, and that purpose is often compelled in your suffering for righteousness's sake. Trust Him today, and He will bring you through for His glory.

GOD IS NEAR

In Ezekiel 48:35, God speaks through His prophet to the children of Israel. He describes the division of the land given to His children by tribe, highlights the boundaries, and states who is to occupy the gates of the city. He names the city "The Lord is Near"—Jehovah Shammah in Hebrew.

God is ever-present wherever you are and in every situation of your life. Would you permit Him to intervene in your life right now? Absolute freedom is found only in Him. Where He is, there is liberty.

Chapter Twenty-Nine:
Finishing Well

Like Job, the Apostle Paul suffered for the sake of Christ, Yet he states:

> But none of these things move me, neither count I my life
> dear unto myself, so that I might finish my course with joy,
> and the ministry, which I have received of the Lord Jesus,
> to testify the gospel of the grace of God. (Acts 20:24, KJV)

In 2 Timothy 4:9–22, Paul shares some salient principles he employed in his dying days. First, the only way to die joyfully is to die fulfilling all that God requires of you. In other words, your joy will be fulfilled when you have obeyed all of God's commands and instructions, and solved problems He intended for you to solve. Do not die until you have fulfilled all of God's purposes for your life. Death cannot seize you if you're willing to fulfill God's purpose for your life and are obedient to His call. Death has no power unless God allows it.

Second, we must learn to hear from God to know His will for our lives. This ensures that when we pray, we do so according to His will and purpose for our lives. God can use anything to stop you from destroying your life. The situations God uses are unlike any other; they are not unto destruction, but unto redemption. In order not to lose heaven, God sometimes has to prevent you from going astray. God will use anything, such as sickness, disease, or even lack to keep you from a continuous path of destruction.

Third, don't judge your Christian life based on your present situation. Don't base your faith on your improvement or lack thereof, because you might be judging too soon, not remembering that God is faithful to His promises. A good soldier knows how to endure hardship. If you honor God when situations seem hopeless, God will honor you even more. Your reward will be greater. The key is to know that God rewards those who diligently seek him.

Epilogue

The call of God to suffer for the sake of Christ, even unto death, is a call into "the great unknown," where we may stumble in the process and even fail along the way. However, it is a sacrificial call to follow in the footsteps of Jesus. Where one's faith in God is tested and must be found to be triumphant.

Jesus overcame worldly temptations, so we are able to overcome through faith in Him. In referring to us, willing followers of Christ, the Word of God says: *"They overcame him* [the devil and his fallen angels] *by the blood of the Lamb and by the word of their testimony; they did not love their lives so much as to shrink from death"* (Revelation 12:11). *"For everyone born of God overcomes the world. This is the victory that has overcome the world, even our faith. Who is it that overcomes the world? Only the one who believes that Jesus is the Son of God"* (1 John 5:4–5).

God has provided the most certain witness to His Word through His Son, Jesus Christ. It's our responsibility to believe in the Son of God to have this witness in us. *"This is he that came by water and blood, even Jesus Christ; not by water only, but by water and blood. And it is the Spirit that beareth witness, because the Spirit is truth"* (1 John 5:6, KJV). The testimony is that God has given eternal life to those who believe in His Son.

As we keep our eyes upon Jesus, He allows us to walk upon the waters of life with all its vicissitudes. We learn how to keep our eyes above the waves. As we turn our eyes upon Jesus and look steadfastly into His wonderful face, our situations will be nothing compared to the glory and grace that we will receive from him. We are called to suffer for His sake, and only then will we be able to reign with Him in glory. Without any physical death, there will be no resurrection. Our end will be greater in the new dispensation of God's glory.

We must know for sure that it is God's perfect will for us to be healed when we're sick. Sickness is a result of the curse, or the fall of Adam. But Jesus came to destroy the works of the evil one.

"For as in Adam all die, even so in Christ shall all be made alive. And so it is written, The first man Adam was made a living soul; the last Adam was made a quickening spirit" (1 Corinthians 15:22, 45).

Jesus, the last Adam, came that we might have life and have it more abundantly. However, it's important to recognize that God uses the base things (foolish things) to confound the wise. In other words, God will use anything for our own good if He deems it necessary. He allowed Paul's "thorn in the flesh" to continue so that His grace might be sufficient for him. God allows situations in our lives to keep us on track. Paul even acknowledged that the "thorn in the flesh" was given to buffet him, or keep him humble.

God allows trial, tribulations, and suffering in our lives for many reasons. Some are to test, to prune, to work eternal weight of glory, and to share in His suffering. God is indeed a good Father. He loves us with an everlasting love, and He works all things for our good.

Be encouraged, pray without ceasing, watch out for the enemy, practice God's presence in your life, and be at peace with Him, yourself, and others as long as it is possible to do so. Rejoice in your tribulations, knowing that God is on your side working things out and making you into His masterpiece. He is shaping you, bringing out the true you, which is in Him. As you share in His suffering, rest assured that you will share in His glory. When Christ shall appear, you shall appear with Him in glory.

"For this corruptible must put on incorruption, and this mortal must put on immortality." (1 Corinthians 15:53 KJV). For this to happen, we must pass from death to life through resurrection.

Those not belonging to Jesus Christ will face a different destiny. Those who die in their sins shall not see God, but eternal damnation will be their portion. Repent now of your sins. Acknowledge Jesus Christ as your Savior and make Him Lord of your life. When this happens, a time of refreshing will come upon you, and His presence will flood your life. Healing and deliverance will be the hallmark of your life through the salvation of our Lord Jesus Christ. Heaven and eternal life will now be yours for sure. If you are a sinner in need of a Savior, just repeat this prayer:

"Dear Lord God, I confess my sins before you. I repent for disobeying you for most of my life. I acknowledge that you have sent Jesus Christ, your Son, to die on the cross for me and that He rose so that I can have eternal life. Thank you for saving my soul and rescuing me from my sins, in Jesus's name. I claim all the rights belonging to me as one of your children, and I receive my healing and deliverance now in Jesus's name."

About the Authors

Glendon Watson is an ordained chaplain in Canada and co-host of the television program *At the Cross Live* on Yes TV. He is presently pursuing doctoral studies in biblical theology. He is a certified project manager and has practiced engineering for over twenty-five years. He is a counseling and deliverance minister who desires to see God's children liberated to do the work of the Lord Jesus Christ. He is the author of *Demons and Devils, How They Enter*, published in 2015.

Maureen Watson is a psychological associate in supervised practice, as well as a certified social worker in Canada. She is pursuing her doctoral studies in biblical theology with her husband. Additionally, she works with her husband in the prayer and deliverance ministry at Global Kingdom Ministries, Toronto, where they are members. They are blessed with a daughter, Latoya.

Printed in Canada